PENNSYLVANIA
MOUNTAIN
LANDMARKS

Pennsylvania Mountain Landmarks

VOLUME 5

Jeffrey R. Frazier

an imprint of Sunbury Press, Inc.
Mechanicsburg, PA USA

an imprint of Sunbury Press, Inc.
Mechanicsburg, PA USA

Copyright © 2025 by Jeffrey R. Frazier.
Cover Copyright © 2025 by Sunbury Press, Inc.

Sunbury Press supports copyright. Copyright fuels creativity, encourages diverse voices, promotes free speech, and creates a vibrant culture. Thank you for buying an authorized edition of this book and for complying with copyright laws. Except for the quotation of short passages for the purpose of criticism and review, no part of this publication may be reproduced, scanned, or distributed in any form without permission. You are supporting writers and allowing Sunbury Press to continue to publish books for every reader. For information contact Sunbury Press, Inc., Subsidiary Rights Dept., PO Box 548, Boiling Springs, PA 17007 USA or legal@sunburypress.com.

For information about special discounts for bulk purchases, please contact Sunbury Press Orders Dept. at (855) 338-8359 or orders@sunburypress.com.

To request one of our authors for speaking engagements or book signings, please contact Sunbury Press Publicity Dept. at publicity@sunburypress.com.

FIRST CATAMOUNT PRESS EDITION: December 2025

Set in Adobe Garamond | Interior design by Crystal Devine | Cover design by Lawrence Knorr. Cover photo by author. | Edited by Lawrence Knorr.

Publisher's Cataloging-in-Publication Data
Names: Frazier, Jeffrey R., author.
Title: Pennsylvania mountain landmarks volume 5 / Jeffrey R. Frazier.
Description: First trade paperback edition. | Mechanicsburg, PA : Catamount Press, 2025.
Summary: As in the first four volumes of this series, volume 5 introduces all new mountain landmarks along with the legends and folktales that surround them. Likewise, there are directions to assist those who may want to find and personally explore these unusual and inaccessible places.
Identifiers: ISBN : 979-8-88819-383-9 (paperback).
Subjects: NATURE / Ecosystems & Habitats / Mountains | HISTORY / United States / State & Local / Middle Atlantic (DC, DE, MD, NJ, NY, PA) | SPORTS & RECREATION / Hiking.

Designed in the USA
0 1 1 2 3 5 8 13 21 34 55

For the Love of Books!

Cover photo: Fort Gaddis (Fayette County) – See Chapter 7 ("Survivors of Pennsylvania Frontier Days") for more details.

CONTENTS

Acknowledgments — vii
Introduction — 1
Author's Note — 7

1. Chief Tammany's Profile (Monroe County) — 9
2. Book's Indian Mound (Juniata County) — 19
3. Love Rock (Dauphin County) — 28
4. Indian Chief Rock (Blair County) — 36
5. Mysteries of Hawk Mountain (Berks County) — 50
6. Landmarks of Pennsylvania's Frontier Days (Fayette, etc.) — 58
7. Survivors of Pennsylvania's Frontier Days — 80
8. Landmark Place Names — 94
9. Odds and Ends — 112
10. Native American Epitaphs — 130

Bibliography — 153
About the Author — 156

ACKNOWLEDGMENTS

I would like once again to acknowledge my appreciation for the members of the Sunbury Press staff who have made this book and all the others in the *Pennsylvania Mountain Landmarks* series and all those in the *Pennsylvania Fireside Tales* series possible. I am also deeply indebted to all those who have agreed to let me use their photos, and who let me interview them to obtain interesting information about those landmarks included herein.

FIRESIDE COMFORTS

by the author when mourning the death of his two spouses

When the fire dances in the inglenook
and falling snowflakes catch the firelight
Then it's time to give life a look
and let thoughts come where they might

The cold winds blow and rattle the panes
the trees creak and groan like ghosts with chains
Branches claw and tear the fabric of night
but there is something secure about firelight

As smoke curls up the chimney in a lazy way
and snowfall makes the air white and blurry
Hear the grandfather clock count off the day
but don't let your thoughts turn to woe and worry

Orange sparks fly and yellow flames rise, then fall
while the winds howl like a panther's call
Snowdrifts rise to a dreadful height
but there is something secure about firelight

Inside a lonely cabin by a troubled stream
a tired old patriarch gazes into the fire
He thinks of his life and a broken dream
Of a lost love and unrequited desire

The fire is dying and leaves only coals
the old man nods and mourns unattained goals
He is saddened by what he has lost in the fight
but there is something secure about firelight

He sleeps by the fire all night long
and dreams of meeting his lost love in the sky
Rested and peaceful, he bursts into song
secure and warm he hears the wind sigh

The ashes of the fire lie dormant and cold
but inside his heart he no longer feels old
He remembers the young girl who gave him his might
Yes indeed, there is something secure about firelight

INTRODUCTION

After completing *Pennsylvania Mountain Landmarks Volume 4*, it turned out that it was much longer than anticipated, and so my publisher agreed it should be split into two volumes. This *Volume 5* is therefore the result of that decision. As it turned out, however, after the pages needed for a *Volume 4* of sufficient size were taken from the original text, there were not enough *Volume 5* pages left to satisfy Sunbury Press publishing guidelines.

This deficiency therefore required that more interesting Pennsylvania landmarks be identified, located, visited, and photographed. That kind of research has always been a pleasure for me, and so I searched the internet and delved into my files and notes to find unique landmarks which were unusual, but which also had interesting historical backgrounds and were colored by legendary lore.

The investigations proved to be fruitful, and as a result the reader will herein find landmarks that are just as interesting, and some even more so, than those written about in the first four volumes.

Similarly, many of the landmarks in *Volume 5* are like those in *Volume 4* in that they have deep-rooted connections to Native American culture and lore. It is a link that indicates, in my opinion, that these places were of as much interest to those aboriginals as they are to us today. They proved to be as awe-inspiring and as mysterious to them as we find them to be at the present time.

And as in us, these places of mystery undoubtedly evoked a longing in the Natives to understand the origins of these unique spots and to know the stories behind their roots. That this is indeed the case can be seen in the legends the Indians had about such locations. Their accounts are colorful and entertaining, a testament to the skills of their storytellers, but also a reflection of the places themselves.

Unique landmarks like this have associations that are far more ancient in origin than other landmarks recorded in the Pennsylvania Mountain Landmarks series. The reason for that is because of their deep-rooted links to the Native Americans who had settled this land long before the first European colonists arrived on our shores. Such colorful ties are not surprising however when you consider that these landmarks are ancient. They predate the humans who first saw them; were here when humankind began to explore the dark recesses where these awe-inspiring places can still be found today.

One of the most common characteristics of the sites is that their rocks are piled in monumental grandeur as if they are memorials to a grander race of men. They are reminders of a time when Native Americans believed the natural world was ruled by fairies, sprites, and otherworldly beings that were all as real to the Indian as wind, rain, and fire.

Science has overruled those quaint ideas, so that today we appreciate these places for their grand scenic effects, rather than for their associations with otherworldly ideas of any kind. Consequently, it seems appropriate to reintroduce this pleasure-land to those who like to explore the many trails and mountain byways Pennsylvania has to offer.

To do that, and to aid all lovers of the outdoors who may want to make the explorations, I have included driving directions and GPS coordinates to all the unusual and inaccessible landmarks heralded in each of the *Pennsylvania Mountain Landmarks* volumes, including this one.

Since this is the last in the five-volume *Pennsylvania Mountain Landmarks* series, I would like to direct readers to some of my favorite landmarks mentioned in all those previous volumes. That is not a particularly easy task for me, any more than it is to respond to readers' queries as to which story is my favorite out of all those I've written about in my eight-volume *Pennsylvania Fireside Tales* series, also published by Sunbury Press.

In both instances I am hard-pressed to single out any one story or landmark since each one has its own unique charm, appeal, or sylvan beauty. Nonetheless, in the case of the landmarks, I will mention favorites from each of the five volumes of this series, with the caveat that this is in no way intended to detract from the exhilaration that can be found when paying a visit to the others.

Moreover, I am convinced the best way to make these excursions is by hiking up to them. By taking the pedestrian routes, you can enjoy nature to its fullest. This way you can experience every scenic vista, enjoy every cloud shape in an azure-blue sky, share the woods with every wild animal you see, enjoy the songs of every bird you hear, and be rewarded with the colors of every wildflower that decorates the trail along which you travel. It is enough to draw us all to lofty mountain tops and to rushing streams cascading down mountain glens. But I digress, and so to add to the enticements I will mention some of my favorite picturesque landmarks.

Starting with *Pennsylvania Mountain Landmarks Volume 1*, I am partial to the chapter on "Picture Rocks" in Lycoming County. The reason is that the interesting profile of an Indian chief can be seen here along the rock cliffs, and also because of the almost-forgotten burial site of an Indian chief and his maid that lies on the mountaintop above the rock canvas where Native Americans once carved strange shapes whose meaning was known only to them.

Also in *Volume 1* is another one of my favorite places that has an unusual nature. In the chapter titled "Boxcar Rocks" is a description of one of the most impressive "rock cities" in the state. Located in Lebanon County, its large, boxcar-sized rocks piled one upon the other all along the ridgetop is a favorite place for rock-climbing enthusiasts to ply their craft.

Included in *Pennsylvania Mountain Landmarks Volume 2* is a chapter titled "Lochabar," which, in my humble opinion, describes one of the most quintessential mountain landmarks in the entire state. Located in Lycoming County, the mysteries this ancient manor house holds are profound. They include that of a silver medallion from President James Madison to each Indian chief in the area, and the enigma of Lochabar's actual "skeleton in the closet." Why the medal was seemingly discarded on the Bald Eagle Mountain, which rises above the old homestead, is a complete mystery. Likewise, but an even greater puzzle, is why the body of a lone Hessian soldier was walled up in one corner of the basement, his skeleton only discovered a century later.

In that same volume is a chapter titled "A Timely Reminder." Proving that the past is really not that far away, this Union County landmark is another true link to the colonial era. The unusual engraving of a clock face, carved into a rectangular stone seen under the roof apex at the east side of the beautiful stone farmhouse built in 1795, causes all who see it to stop and wonder. Its story is not well known, but it is a reminder of the fortitude and tenacity it took to settle and remain in the area during a time of bloody warfare with Native American tribesmen. It is well worth a visit for those wishing to feel a greater connection to those people and that time.

Pennsylvania Mountain Landmarks Volume 3 has two sites that are among my favorites. The first is described in the chapter titled "Hexenkopf Rock." Translated from the Pennsylvania Dutch into English, the title means "Witch's Head." This spot in Berks County is steeped in supernatural tales of witchcraft and hexerei that were once so popular and implicitly believed by the local populace. The profile of an old-time witch that can be seen on the rocks here only reinforces the idea that it once was, and is still to some today, a place of mystery and a spot to avoid, especially at night!

The second place in *Volume 3* I'd like to mention is described in the chapter titled "Bilger's Rocks." Located in Clearfield County, it is another "rock city" whose many dark and winding passageways, overgrown with massive roots, lead to shadowy "rooms," whose names like the "Devil's Dungeon" and the "Devil's Dining Room" make it an uninviting place. Moreover, its many carvings and formations, both manmade and natural, create a feeling of stepping back into a time of prehistory; they induce an impression, however unlikely, that even dinosaurs might have once sheltered here.

In *Pennsylvania Mountain Landmarks Volume 4* the chapter titled "Indian Steps Revisited" holds a special place in my list of favorites because it presents a plausible theory explaining the origins of the stone stairway that spans Tussey Mountain between Huntingdon and Centre Counties. Once thought to have been constructed by Native Americans, this chapter debunks that notion and offers a more reasonable explanation.

Also in *Volume 4* is the chapter titled "Witches' Hill," which delves into the events which led to the names of two such spots bearing that same title—one in Berks County and one in Somerset County. Both spots are associated with tales of local witches who were once believed to exercise extraordinary powers due to their pledges to serve the demon of the underworld. Their stories are throwbacks to a time when people were convinced that such things were possible and feared the old crones as a result.

Finally, in this volume, the "Love Rock" chapter describes a rock formation in Dauphin County whose story has a romantic twist. Although the indentations on the rock face provide some support for its legend, historical evidence is lacking.

Likewise in *Volume 5*, there is a lack of evidence behind the claim that an Indian maiden is buried along Nichols Run Road north of Jersey Shore in Lycoming County. In the chapter titled "Native American Epitaphs," I tried to find any evidence that an Indian maiden is indeed buried at the place along here that is marked by a gravestone engraved with the words "Shawana the Last Indian Girl of the West Branch Valley." Although there seems to be some evidence to support the burial claims, there does not seem to be enough to confirm the maiden's actual name.

With those tantalizing places presented to you, I hope you will enjoy finding them and exploring them as much as I have. They are part of Pennsylvania's colorful landscape that offers "miles to wander." There are fresh vistas at every turn, new delights that surprise us when least expected, and gentle breezes that seem to revive forgotten and imaginative stories of the long ago which add zest to the scenes that unfold. Enjoy our natural heritage and vow to preserve it for our children and grandchildren so that they will do the same for theirs.

AUTHOR'S NOTE

In the Introduction to my *Pennsylvania Fireside Tales Volume 7*, I mentioned that in my travels I had the pleasure of experiencing some fabulous mountain vistas all over the state and listed my favorites. However, much to my delight in traveling across Pennsylvania to visit and to take photos of the places included in this volume, I discovered some vistas that, much to my surprise and pleasure, excel those I listed previously.

And like those I mentioned in *Pennsylvania Fireside Tales Volume 7*, I wanted to share these new ones with my readers so they could enjoy them also. On the other hand, I share them with a note of caution. Anyone driving along Route 30 between Fort Loudon, Franklin County, and Bedford, Bedford County, will cross the Cove Mountains and will be impressed with the many incredible vistas along here which seem to come one after another.

They are so spectacular, particularly those on the Tuscarora Mountain, that in my opinion they rival those attracting tourists to the Blue Ridge Mountains of Virginia. Consequently, drivers can be easily distracted and so should take extra care to drive carefully.

These views have not, to my surprise, gotten the attention they deserve. Poets have regaled the "Hills of Somerset" in their prose, and writers have praised the mountain panoramas that enthrall travelers in central Pennsylvania, but the ridges of Bedford, Franklin and Fulton Counties await their Bard. Perhaps, someone reading these accolades will be inspired to be that bard, and to write praises to these vistas in much more glorious and shining praise than the humble writer of these lines can hope to do.

CHAPTER 1

CHIEF TAMMANY'S PROFILE

One of the jewels in Pennsylvania's crown of landmarks is the Delaware Water Gap National Recreation Area. It is a place of such natural beauty and rugged landscape that, as of 2022, it was being considered for designation as a United States National Park. Encompassing almost 70,000 acres along a forty-mile stretch on both sides of the Delaware River, it's a place of environmental wonder and a recreational paradise. Among its scenic attractions are hundreds of waterfalls that stream off the Pocono Plateau and into the Delaware River, including the two tallest in Pennsylvania, Dingmans Falls and Raymondskill Falls, a three-tiered cascade that is the tallest in the state and only a few feet shorter than the mighty Niagara Falls in New York State. One of the most visited is Bushkill Falls, tabbed "the Niagara of Pennsylvania" because of its voluminous flow. Here also, the Delaware River forms the boundary line between Pennsylvania and New Jersey as it slices its way through a wild mountain cut between Blue Mountain and Kittatinny Mountain in the Pocono Mountains and into Delaware Bay in the state of Delaware.

The waterway is unique since it is the longest undammed river in the Eastern United States. It has also been called the "Lifeblood of the Northeast" since it provides drinking water for 17 million people, including those living in Philadelphia and in New York City.[1] Considered as having natural, cultural, and recreational values that are a source of enjoyment for

---

1. American Rivers Federation, "Delaware River, Lifeblood of the Northeast," www.americanrivers.org/river/delaware-river.

Penn's Great Treaty With the Indians. Oil painting by Benjamin West. Commissioned by Thomas Penn, son of Pennsylvania's founder, this painting depicts a legendary meeting between William Penn and members of the Lenni Lenape tribe at Shackamaxon on the Delaware River. There is some doubt whether the likeness of the Indian chief in the painting is that of chief Tammany, however, since the painting was done 100 years after the scene it portrays acctually occurred.

present as well as future generations, the waterway was inducted into the National Wild and Scenic Rivers System in 1978.[2] It also has played a part in the nation's colonial history, Washington's crossing at Trenton during the Revolutionary War in 1776 is the most notable example, but it also served as a conduit for settlers entering the region and for industries that grew up along the banks of the river. Moreover, its history goes back even further, since a number of significant Native American archeological sites have been found in the park.

The Native American presence here is also reflected in the names of several peaks at the water gap. Here on the Blue Mountain in Pennsylvania there is Mount Minsi while on the Kittatinny Mountain in New Jersey there is Mount Tammany. Both names have aboriginal origins, with Minsi coming from the name of an Indian tribe that once inhabited the region, and Tammany being the name of one of their most famous chieftains.

---

2. United States Geological Survey, "Delaware Water Gap," Geographic Names Information System, January 28, 2022.

An 1857 lithograph depicting the wampum belt of oyster beads and leather handed to William Penn by the Lenni Lenape at the Great Treaty. The wampum belt was donated by Penn's great grandson to the Historical Society of Pennsylvania in 1857.

The Minsi people were the Wolf clan of the Munsees, which in turn were the Munsee clan of the Algonkians. The chief village of the Minsi was located on the New Jersey side of the river southeast of present-day Milford. They called their village Minisink, signifying "the place of the Minsi," a name that eventually was used to signify both sides of the river north of the water gap.[3] These were the aborigines that had the distinction of being among the first indigenous people to encounter the earliest Europeans who entered the area.

Initial interactions with those settlers were peaceful and cordial, but following the notorious Walking Purchase of 1737, a fraudulent treaty between the Munsee and the sons of William Penn, the Munsee were forced to move from the Minisink about 1740 (more will be said about that later in this chapter). They first settled along the Susquehanna River to the west, but from there they moved further west to join Lenape settlements on the Ohio River. Others who remained in New York eventually became absorbed by the Mohawks in Schoharie County.[4]

Although the Munsees had assigned their own name to the water gap, calling it "Buck-ka-buck-ka" or "mountains butting opposite of each other,"[5] they also had their own name for the river, calling it Lenape Wihittuck, or "the rapid stream of the Lenape."[6] Nonetheless, the colonists decided to name it after one of their own. The name they chose was De La Warr, in honor of Thomas West, 3rd Baron De La Warr, (1577–1618), an English nobleman and first royal governor of the Virginia Colony whose deeds of

---

3. Doctor George P. Donehoo, *Indian Villages and Place Names in Pennsylvania*, 108.
4. Frederick Webb Hodge, *Handbook of American Indians North of Mexico*, 385 ff.
5. Donehoo, ibid, 57.
6. Reverend John Heckewelder and Peter S. Du Ponceau, "Names Which the Lenni Lenape or Delaware Indians, etc.," *Transactions of the American Philosophical Society*, Volume 4, article 11, 351–96.

View of Mount Tammany and Tammany's Face from Point of Gap Overlook at Delaware Water Gap National Recreation Area in Monroe County (Taken by the author in July of 2024)

valor were credited with saving the settlers at Jamestown from annihilation by Powhatan warriors during the Anglo-Powhatan war of 1609–1614.[7]

Over time the English title for the river came to be spelled Delaware, and as a result it was eventually used as a collective designation for all Lenni Lenape who inhabited the basins of the Delaware River, Susquehanna River, and lower Hudson River. That description followed them wherever they went, even to the American Midwest and to Canada, and it remains with us today.[8]

Likewise, there is another Delaware name that has also come down to us because it was neither forgotten nor discarded by our American ancestors, and it survives in various forms, perhaps to remind us of the injustices once inflicted upon the Delawares. The appellation of note is that of the Lenni Lenape chieftain who bore the name Tammany and for whom Mount Tammany on the Blue Mountain on the New Jersey side of the Delaware Water Gap is named. Sometimes also referred to as Tamanend

---

7. Albert Frederick Pollard, "West, Thomas (1577-1618)," *Dictionary of National Biography 1885–1900, Volume 60*, 344–45.
8. Clinton A. Weslager, *The Delaware Indians: A History*, 47–50.

Close up of Tammany's Face (indicated by the arrow) on Mount Tammany (Taken from Point of Gap Overlook by the author in July of 2024)

and Taminent, he was not only highly regarded by his Native American peers but also held in great respect by colonial Pennsylvanians as well, mainly because of his role as a diplomat and also as an interpreter between the two widely different cultures.

His virtues as a decent human being were noted by Moravian missionary Reverend John Heckewelder, a staunch friend of the Delawares who lived among them for thirty years. According to Heckewelder, "The name of Tamanend is held in highest veneration by all the Indians. Of all the chiefs and great men which the Lenape nation ever had, he stands foremost on the list. He was an ancient Delaware chief who never had an equal. He was in the highest degree, endowed with wisdom, virtue, prudence, charity, affability, meekness, hospitality; in short with every good and noble qualification that any human being may possess."[9]

Tamamend's most famous role as a mediator between the Lenni Lenape of the Minisink and the colonial Quaker government was as a signer of the famous treaty between William Penn and the chiefs of the Lenni Lenape in 1683 (most recently thought to have occurred in June of that year). Held

---

9. C. Hale Sipe, *The Indian Chiefs of Pennsylvania*, 57.

under a large elm tree at Shackamaxon, chief village of the Delaware Turtle Clan along the Delaware River and within the limits of present-day Penn Treaty Park in Philadelphia, it would later be described as "the only treaty never sworn to and never broken."[10]

The agreement was formulated with the highest of intentions, Penn declaring: "We meet on the broad pathway of good faith and good will; no advantage shall be taken on either side, but all shall be openness and love. We are the same as if one man's body was to be divided into two parts we are of one flesh and one blood."[11]

Tammany, as head chief of the Turtle Clan, presided over the council fires of the three clans of the Delaware Nation and so could serve as their spokesman in addressing Penn's comments.[12] Therefore, as such, he in turn nobly replied: "We will live in love with William Penn and his children as long as the creeks and rivers run and while the sun, moon and stars endure."[13]

The treaty would later be referred to by some historians as "The Great Treaty," probably because it was thought to be as important in the history of human relations as that of England's Magna Carta; that country's "Great Charter"—a pact between King John and his barons, who were fed up with the King's absolute authoritarian rule. Penn's treaty did not prove to be as long lived as the Great Charter, however, ending with the Penns Creek massacre on October 16, 1755.

It was a miracle that Penn's "Great Treaty" lasted almost 75 years, given the way the Delaware were disrespected by Penn's sons after their father died. Evicted from their lands after the fraudulent Walking Purchase of 1737, the uprooted Indians harbored an intense hatred of the Penns and of all those who began settling on their lands. There is no doubt that the Walking Purchase was an egregious land swindle of epic proportions. The Delaware, in their trusting and naïve ways, had expected the men appointed by Penn's sons to walk the allotted day's time for claiming the land that was to be covered by the so-called "walking purchase." However, the Penns not only instructed their men to run all day but also cleared a trail so they could do so unhindered.

---

10. Ibid, 60.
11. Ibid.
12. C. Hale Sipe, *The Indian Wars of Pennsylvania*, 73–74.
13. C. Hale Sipe, *The Indian Chiefs of Pennsylvania*, 60.

Bushkill Falls – the "Niagara of Pennsylvania." Delaware Water Gap National Recreation Area in Monroe County (taken by the author in 2023).

As a result of the large territory claimed by the sons of William Penn through their counterfeit Walking Purchase, the Delawares were instructed to vacate the lands that they had held for decades. Appeals for help to their Iroquois brethren of the Six Nations fell upon deaf ears, even though the Delaware, in the terms of the treaty, had been promised that they could remain in their cabins and on their farms. However, Chief Tammany could do nothing, perhaps because the colonists harbored so much resentment against the Delawares, never forgetting their bloody raids on their settlements during the war years of the mid to late 1770s.

Here Tammany spent his remaining years and became a decidedly different man. His efforts to persuade Pennsylvania's government and the Iroquois Confederation to allow the Delaware to settle along the Susquehanna River were unsuccessful. He was further disillusioned during the French and Indian war of the 1750s when Lenape attacks on Pennsylvania settlements became a regular occurrence. His despondency was compounded in 1757 when a settler shot and killed one of his sons. Then the construction of frontier forts along the Delaware, Fort Hamilton in 1756 and Fort Penn during the Revolutionary War of the 1770s, undoubtedly

Dingman's Falls – one of the most impressive water falls to be found at Delaware Water Gap National Recreation Area in Monroe County (taken by the author in July of 2024).

added to Tammany's conviction that it was the unquenchable desire of the ever-more-numerous settlers "To drive us all out and possess themselves of our land."[14]

His life at this stage was filled with anger, remorse, and a sense of failure, and Tammany turned to liquor as a source of comfort, often drinking to excess. It was a sad ending for a man who up until then was, in Heckewelder's words, "a stranger to everything that was bad."[15] He died in late 1760, but his memory lives on in places named after him, including the borough of Tatamy in Northampton County, and Mount Tammany in New Jersey.

It has also been suggested that the stone profile on Mount Tammany is that of the great chieftain, and that it was carved there by his Native American compatriots to honor him. On the other hand, if that is true then it has not withstood the ravages of time too well, requiring a great degree of imagination to see any profile whatsoever there today. More than likely, it is just part of the natural landscape here, but as such it still memorializes the life of a courageous and honorable man.

---

14. James H. Merrell, *Into the American Woods: Negotiators on the Pennsylvania Frontier*, 293.
15. C. Hale Sipe, *The Indian Chiefs of Pennsylvania*, 57.

LOCATION: Chief Tammany's profile is located in the Delaware Water Gap National Recreation area of the Pocono Mountains of Monroe County, Pennsylvania, and the Kittatinny Mountains of Warren County, New Jersey.

DD GPS COORDINATES: 40°58'01.5"N, 75°07'17.1"W

DRIVING DIRECTIONS: From Stroudsburg, take Route 611 Southeast and continue on Route 611 into the town of Delaware Water Gap. Turn right onto Main Street in the town and follow it out onto Route 611. Follow Route 611 out to Point of Gap Overlook to view Mount Tammany and its Indian Head (profile of Chief Tammany).

NOTES:

1. There is yet another remarkable reminder of the great Delaware chieftain Tammany that can be seen today. In Drexel University's Atwater Kent collection formerly housed in the Philadelphia History Museum, there is a belt of wampum beads believed to have been given to William Penn by the Lenape Indians during the "Great Treaty" ceremony held under the Shackamaxon elm in 1683. Depicted upon this token of friendship from the Delaware to William Penn are two men clasping hands: the larger one, thought by some to represent William Penn wearing his large Quaker hat, and the smaller one hatless and representing a Native American (Perhaps Chief Tammany as some claim, but that's not certain).[16]

2. Grafts of the Shackamaxon elm were taken before it was felled by a storm in 1810 and grafted to other elms. Though thought to be rare, some of these so-called Penn Treaty elms are said to still be alive and well. An obelisk was erected to mark the spot of the original elm and stands there today as a notable landmark in Penn Treaty Park. The wood from the original Penn Treaty elm was even used to create souvenir objects and furniture.[17]

---

16. Kerr Houston, "Re-reading Wampum: The Penn Treaty Belt and Indeterminate Iconographies," *Panorama: Journal of the Association of Historians of American Art*, Spring 2023 (9.1), https://doi.org/10.24926/24716839.17266.

17. Richard Naples, "Native American Heritage Month: Penn Treaty Wampum Belts," *Unbound*, Smithsonian Libraries and Archives, November 23, 2016.

3. In 1738 William Penn's sons, Thomas, John, and Richard, allotted a 325-acre parcel to Tammany in the Lehigh Valley in appreciation for successfully keeping the peace between the colonists and the Delaware up until that time.[18] That was one year after the notorious Walking Purchase and so perhaps the Penns hoped their gift would motivate Tammany to continue to be the peacekeeper he had so effectively proved to be in the past. That worked for almost twenty years, until the Penns Creek Massacre in 1755.

---

18. Robert S. Grumet, editor, *Northeastern Indian Lives 1632–1816*, 258 ff.

CHAPTER 2

BOOK'S INDIAN MOUND

Of all the colonial wars that scorched and burned the once-verdant landscape of Pennsylvania, there was another forgotten war that has been overshadowed by them. On the other hand, it cannot actually be called a war since it is best described as just a single battle. Moreover, where it happened, when it happened, and even if it happened at all remains a mystery. History has not provided answers to those questions. However, as is often the case when history is lacking, folktales and legends pick up the slack and venture off on their own.

In that uncertain realm, this folktale of a single battle between Shawnees and Delawares is called the Grasshopper War. Despite that misnomer, the legend does have one distinction, which is best described by John Witthoft, recognized authority on Pennsylvania archeology and anthropology.

The Grasshopper War, Witthoft wrote, is "a distinctively American Indian story, which has become part of the oral tradition of the White community."[1]

Witthoft proposed that the legend originated with the Delaware and Shawnee tribes as a way to explain why, when they had once come together to become one people with a common language, "they had separated and whose languages had changed."[2]

He then went on to suggest that this same folktale became widely accepted in the culture of colonial frontiersmen as a way to explain why there were places where they found so many arrowheads, tomahawks, and other evidence of a large tribal battleground. Or, as Witthoft put

---
1. John Witthoft, "The Grasshopper War in Lenape Land," *Pennsylvania Archeologist 16 (1946)*, 91–94.
2. Ibid.

it, "the presence of a conspicuous archeological site as an alleged Indian battleground."[3]

Witthoft also stated that in Pennsylvania "Within the area of original Delaware settlement, this tale is only known from Durham Township in northeastern Bucks County."[4]

I have to take exception to that claim, however, based upon my own travels and investigations. One thing I learned over my many years of research is that folktales and legends are not reliable sources to depend upon when deciding whether the events to which they refer actually happened. They could instead just be a recollection of a tall tale of a particular day and age. Moreover, even historical sources tend to fall short in that regard as well. That is especially true when the same account travels; that is, when it is found in different widely-separated spots.

In such cases, it is difficult, if not impossible, to determine where the original event may have occurred, let alone if it happened at all. And therein lies the problem with trying to authenticate the tale of the so-called Grasshopper War. It is a story that seems to have such an historic appeal that, besides Bucks County, three other Pennsylvania counties have also claimed it as their own. One of them is found in Wyoming County, one in Luzerne County, and the third in Juniata County.

In the Wyoming Valley of Wyoming County, there is a spot known locally as Honeypot Knob. It is a small hillock so-named from the fact that on the knob's peak is a bowl-like depression in which honeysuckle vines grew profusely during the summer months and where numerous bee hives overflowing with honey could once be found. Although a place of natural beauty, it was here, according to local legend, that the "Grasshopper War" took place one summer day. However, no historical records mention such a battle, and details about it are preserved only in the area's legendary lore.

According to the Wyoming Valley version of the legend, one summer day some Shawnee women and their children were peacefully gathering fruit from bushes and trees which grew at the foot of a small elevation the early colonial settlers would later call Honeypot Knob. Not too far away a group of Delaware women and their children were picking fruit as well.

Usually such a scene would have been a pleasant one; warm summer breezes filling the air with the fragrance of honeysuckle flowers, dusky

---
3. Ibid.
4. Ibid.

Copse of trees surrounding Book's Indian Mound monument, located along Licking Creek in Beale Township of Juniata County.

Indian maidens busily picking berries from blackberry or huckleberry bushes and laughing Indian children finding delight in even the simplest of nature's creations.

All seemed contented and peaceful until one of the children found a large grasshopper and began playing with it. The insect attracted the attention of a child from the other tribe who wanted to play with it also. However, the finder of the bug was not willing to share it, and a squabble broke out.

Soon the mothers were involved, and an argument started over which group had territorial rights to this particular area. Then more children and women joined the fight until they all had become embroiled in the fray. At this point the warriors returned from a peaceful hunting trip, and they immediately jumped into the melee to protect their families.

The contest turned out to be a long and bloody affair, and, according to the legend, when the sun finally sank behind the hills, the last rays of sunlight fell upon a battlefield strewn with corpses, which were mostly those of the finest Shawnee warriors. It was as a result of this victory, claims the legend, that the Delawares were able to expel the Shawnees from the valley.[5]

As noted, there is no historical record of such a battle, nor is there any physical evidence to support it. Consequently, it is the lack of that proof that makes the Wyoming County location suspect as far as its claims for being the place where the Grasshopper War actually happened in Pennsylvania. Moreover, also as noted, there is some competition in that regard, since three other counties contend that the true place where this notorious battle took place was on their soil.

One of those is the aforementioned site in Bucks County, another is in Luzerne County where a Delaware Indian village once stood near the mouth of Wapwallopen Creek, and the third is along the banks of Licking Creek in Juniata County where evidence of a Tuscarora village has been found.

Supporters of the assertion that the Grasshopper War occurred at the Bucks County site do seem to make a good case for that claim, as do the claimants for their sites in Luzerne and Wyoming Counties. In the end, however, none of those three groups have come forth with physical evidence that seems to support their argument. On the other hand, that is what sets the Juniata County site apart from the others.

Up in Beale Township in the Academia area of Juniata County, the legend of the Grasshopper War has been told and retold for almost two centuries. Here the belief is that the great battle took place along the banks of Licking Creek. In this case, however, the combatants are said to be Delawares and Tuscaroras, instead of Delawares and Shawnees. Regardless of that difference, there is some convincing evidence at the site that supports the idea that such a battle may have once indeed taken place here.

Standing in a small copse of trees, in the middle of a field along Licking Creek, there is a granite monument with an engraved memorial stone attached to its face. The lettering on that memorial stone indicates that standing here at one time was a large Native American burial mound. However, because of human impact, no such mound can be seen at this place today. Disregarding its significance to the Native American culture, early farmers dug away at the mound and used its contents for fertilizer.

---

5. Sherman Day, *Historical Collections of the State of Pennsylvania*, 432.

View of Book's Indian Mound monument hidden in the copse of trees.

Likewise, students from the nearby Tuscarora Academy dug into it when searching for Indian artifacts. Consequently, its original size, estimated to be up to fifteen feet high, thirty feet long, and twenty feet wide, was greatly diminished.[6]

Its designation as a Native American burial mound was confirmed when a large number of skeletons were found buried in the mound when archeologists from the Pennsylvania Historical Commission conducted a scientific excavation of it in 1929. Today the mound, named the Book Indian Mound since it stood on farmland owned by the Book family, is protected from further vandalism by Pennsylvania law, and because in 1986 it was added to the National Register of Historic Places.[7]

The archeologists who excavated the site in 1929 discovered 22 skeletons buried therein, which seemed to prove to some that there may have been a large battle here after all. This also led many to believe that if this was so, then the legendary claim that this was the place of the infamous Grasshopper War may also be true. After all, hadn't this battle involved

---

6. Franklin Ellis and Austin N. Hungerford, editors, *History of that Part of the Susquehanna and Juniata Valleys Embraced in the Counties of Mifflin, Juniata, Perry, Union, and Snyder in the Commonwealth of Pennsylvania Volume 1*, 790–91.

7. National Park Service website, "National Trust Sites in Pennsylvania."

Close up of Book's Indian Mound monument.

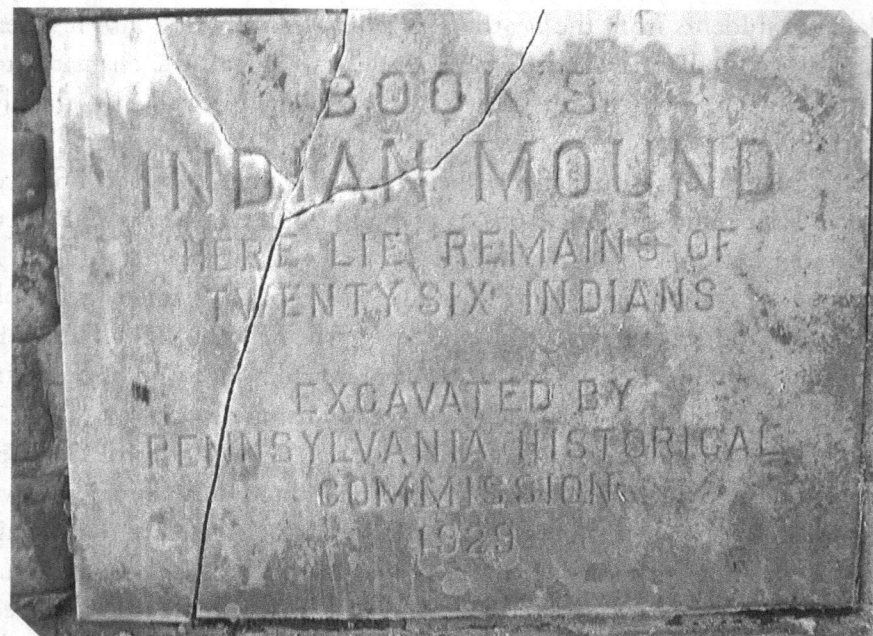
Inscription on Book's Indian Mound monument.

a large number of warriors, and hadn't a large number of them perished in that violent skirmish? If so, then wouldn't the slain have been buried together in a common grave? Convincing thoughts, but evidence would suggest otherwise.

At first it seemed like a plausible argument, but on the other hand that grandiloquent historian of the Juniata Valley, Uriah J. Jones, when acknowledging the existence of the mound and its legend of a large Indian battle occurring here, goes on to say that although "tradition speaks of battles among the Indians, the tradition is so vague and unsatisfactory that we may omit any further mention of them."[8]

The reason for that ambiguity is not surprising when archeological evidence is considered. That evidence indicates that the mound was built over 500 years or more before the time of Columbus. Given that antiquity it's possible that any great tribal battle that may have happened here occurred in a time of prehistory and so has been long forgotten. On the other hand, anthropological studies raise doubts that the mound is a mass burial spot at all. The reason for that skepticism is because it's known that large Native American burial mounds like this were not built all at once, but over time. They were used and re-used to bury deceased villagers as the need arose.[9]

These uncertainties leave us in a quandary. Did the Grasshopper War occur at this place or has this folktale been misplaced. Was it ensconced here by early settlers who used it to explain why they found so many Indian arrow points and similar artifacts in the mound. No definite answers to resolve these questions are likely to be forthcoming today. All the photos, skulls, bones, arrow points, bits of pottery, and other artifacts discovered during the dig in 1929 have been lost; can no longer be found by the Pennsylvania Historical Commission! Likewise, most of the mound itself was destroyed during the 1929 archeological excavation.[10]

Nonetheless, the monument at the destroyed mound still causes us to pause and wonder. It is a situation that frustrates and perplexes historians and folklorists alike. Typical of many legendary accounts, there is always that barrier of gossamer mist that separates the past from the present. It is a veil through which we cannot see; an obstruction that perhaps reminds us that the spirits of the past are better left undisturbed.

---

8. Uriah J. Jones, *History of the Early Settlement of the Juniata Valley*, 76.
9. Juniata County Historical Society Publication, "The Book Indian Mound" based on 1929 articles published in the *Juniata Tribune*.
10. Ibid.

> **LOCATION:** Book's Indian Mound can be found along the banks of Licking Creek on Camp Resort Road in Beale Township, near the community of Beale, in Juniata County.
>
> **DD GPS COORDINATES:** 40°28'44.5"N, 77°30'2.4"W
>
> **DRIVING DIRECTIONS:** Follow Route 22 East out of Lewistown, then turn right onto Route 75 South toward Port Royal. Continue on Route 75 until you can make a right turn onto Ebenezer Church Road. Follow until you can turn right onto Barton Hill Road. At a T intersection, turn left onto Pleasant View Road, and follow until you can turn right onto Indian Mound Road. The Book's Indian Mound will be on the left.

NOTE: The fate of the Book Indian Mound is not unique as far as its leveling and destruction by human hands. There are accounts of many others Pennsylvania mounds which suffered the same fate. Several of the most significant include the Conestoga Mound in Lancaster County; two Monongahela Mounds in Washington County; and the following:

McKees Rocks Mound

Upon its discovery it was considered to be the largest prehistoric mound found in Western Pennsylvania. Located on a high bluff overlooking the confluence of Chartiers Creek and the Ohio River in the borough of McKees Rocks, Allegheny County, it was originally sixteen feet high and had a basal diameter of eighty-five feet. It no longer exists. In the early 1900s, quarrying operations for the rock beneath the bluff slowly destroyed the mound.[11]

Kushkushkee Mound

Though smaller than the McKees Rocks Mound, it was nonetheless an eye-catching landmark. The mound was located along the Mahoning River, on the south side of the present town of Edinburgh and about five miles west of the city of Newcastle, Lawrence County. Earliest reports described it to be "about fifty feet in circumference, and six feet high in the center." Its name was derived from the fact that a Native American village called Kushkushkee once stood at this same spot. Early missionary Christian Frederick Post visited here in 1758, and noted "Kushkushkee is divided into four towns,

---

11. Mark A. McConaughy, "McKees Rocks," *The Blog of the Pennsylvania State Historic Preservation Office*, April 15, 2015.

each at a distance from the others; and the whole consists of about ninety houses, and two hundred able warriors." Up until 1871 the mound was still in perfect condition, but when a group of curious history buffs visited the site that year they found "three-fourths of it had been leveled to the grade of the field surrounding it, which, we were informed, had been done by the owner of the land, with the expectation of finding some hidden treasure." A memory of the Indian town that once stood here is preserved in an historical marker erected by the Pennsylvania Historical Commission, which reads: "Important group of Indian towns on and near site of present New Castle. First inhabited by Senecas; but after 1756 settled chiefly by Delawares from eastern Pennsylvania. Abandoned during Revolutionary War."[12]

Buckaloons Mounds

Located in the Allegheny National Forest of Warren County, several burial mounds were once prominent features at the Native American town of Buckaloons. Located at the junction of Brokenstraw Creek and the Allegheny River, the village was the home of a tribe of Senecas, which were one of the Six Nations of the Iroquois Confederacy. The mounds no longer exist, but their existence is mentioned on the Pennsylvania Historical and Museum Commission Marker that stands here: "A famous Indian village, visited by Celoron in 1749 and destroyed by Brodhead in 1779. Burial mounds excavated here indicate the antiquity of this site."[13]

Sugar Run Mounds

Discovery of eight Native American burial mounds in 1941 verified that as far back as 500 BC that ancient race had occupied present-day Warren County. Excavations of the mounds were done by Civilian Conservation Corps employees and by a crew of Seneca Indians from the Allegheny Reservation, all under the supervision of the Pennsylvania Historical and Museum Commission. The excavations were conducted despite the fact that at that late date all of them had been plowed down almost to ground level by the farmer who owned the land.[14]

---

12. E. M. McConnell, "Account of an Old Indian Village Kushkushkee Near Newcastle, Pennsylvania" *Annual Report of the Board of Regents of the Smithsonian Institution*, 1871. Also: Betty DiRisio Hoover, "Ancient Indian Burial Mound" *Blog of the Lawrence County Historical Society*, May 5, 2014.

13. Inscription on the Pennsylvania Historical and Museum Commission marker for Buckaloons standing at Irvine in Warren County.

14. Mark A. McConaughy and Janet R. Johnson, "Sugar Run Mound and Village: Hopewell/Middle Woodland in Warren County, Pennsylvania," *Foragers and Farmers of the Early and Middle Woodlands Periods in Pennsylvania*, 101-116.

CHAPTER 3

LOVE ROCK

The reader will by now have noticed that many of the landmarks discussed in this volume have deep-rooted connections to the Native Americans who had settled this land long before the first European colonists arrived on our shores. These connections are not surprising, however, when you consider that these landmarks are ancient. They predate the humans who first saw them; were here when humankind began to explore the dark recesses where they stand yet today. Then also consider how Native Americans cultivated and preserved their own myths and legends, many of which were attempts to understand natural events that, to them, could only be understood by a belief that supernatural forces were the cause.

Likewise, the same might be said of their attitude toward certain unique and unusual landmarks that nature has carved out and fashioned from stacks of rocks and on rock ledges. This is especially true if those designs have human characteristics; a trait that aborigines must have been compelled to explain. For several notable examples see the chapter titled "Cast Into Stone" in the author's *Pennsylvania Fireside Tales Volume 3*, the chapter titled "Faces From the Past", in *Pennsylvania Fireside Tales Volume 6*, and "Indian Chief Rock" in this volume.

These Native American legends and myths have proved to be as durable as the rocks they celebrate, and so that is why they still surface from time to time today. I was both surprised and pleased to have found so many of them and to be able to share them with the reader. This is especially true of the story in this chapter, which I find particularly remarkable because it does not appear to be an account invented by settlers who lived at the time

View of Love Rock. The small black circles on the rock at the top left are the pockets that, according to legend, were carved there by the jilted lover who went mad when his intended bride was swept away by a colonial admirer. (Photo courtesy of Michael Meehan.)

the story is said to have occurred. Instead, it seems more apt to be of Native American origins; a legend they told and retold as they sat by the dancing flames of their campfires.

If that is true, then it must also have been a story adopted and revised by early settlers to add their own touches to the narrative. After all, it does not seem probable that the Indians would have tried to preserve the names of the two colonial brothers named in the tale. The settlers, on the other hand, may have been prone to add the names to make the storyline more of their own.

As such, then, this account could be sort of a hybrid; an Indian folktale that was adopted by early colonists and possibly changed to honor some of their forebears. That early settlers would incorporate Native American folktales into their own cultural traditions is not without precedent. However, there is only one other case where this has been proposed, that of the story of the infamous Grasshopper War.

That story recalls how two tribes of aborigines had always lived in peace until one day two children, one from each tribe, got into a dispute over a grasshopper they had discovered along a creek. This childish argument escalated into a full-blown war between the two tribes, until many warriors on both sides had been killed. The tale became widespread and repeated throughout various parts of Pennsylvania, handed down through generations of early settlers who found the story appealing. For full details, see the chapter titled "Book's Indian Mound" in this volume, and also see the chapter titled "Campbell's Ledge" in the author's *Pennsylvania Fireside Tales Volume 3*.

Historian John Witthoft, in a 1953 article appearing in the *Journal of American Folklore*, proposed that the tale of the Grasshopper War "is the only American Indian folktale to become part of the white community's oral tradition."[1] Witthoft also suggested that this happened because it explained in part the substantial number of Indian artifacts found in the areas where a large battle like this was supposed to have occurred.

With these thoughts in mind, it is not out of line to think that the rock landmark we want to consider in this chapter is so unique that it compelled Native American storytellers to come up with an explanation as to why it has the odd characteristics it exhibits. Their story, like that of the Grasshopper War, may have proved just as compelling to white settlers so that they incorporated it into their own oral tradition, with some additions of their own. Conjecture on my part, but not totally out of the question in my humble opinion. But the reader can decide for themselves, as we now begin the story of Love Rock, which I paraphrase from a much-romanticized telling that is the earliest known version on record.

The account begins in New York State, in the years preceding the American Revolution. Among the European immigrants arriving in the Dutch settlement of New Amsterdam, on the southern tip of present-day Manhattan Island, were 24-year-old brothers Harold and William Wingans. Restless by nature, the fraternal twins only stayed there a brief time, then decided to head into the western wilderness together.

They rarely saw another human being; but were so captivated by the natural beauty that surrounded them that they forgot their quest for riches and instead turned to a wilderness life. Hunting, fishing, trapping, and evading Indian war parties became their daily routine, and they eventually wandered southward into Pennsylvania. Here they were even more captivated by the beauty of the mighty Susquehanna River and the valleys it had

---

1. Mention of the Witthoff article was found on page 43 of *It Happened in Mifflin County* by Forest K. Fisher, where he says he found it in a 1953 edition of the *Journal of American Folklore*.

Some young ladies in their Sunday best taking in the view from Love Rock (from an old photo).

carved. Drawn to it, they followed the river until one day they discovered an Indian camp where a small stream emptied into the waterway.

The brothers were natural diplomats and soon had befriended the natives, who welcomed them. After a brief time, their new friends explained to the brothers that they were only a small part of a larger group encamped sixteen miles to the east. They also said they were heading back there to partake in a great feast and that the brothers were welcome to join them.

The brothers, with their natural sense of adventure, accepted the invitation without hesitation, and after a day's travel found themselves in the larger encampment at the foot of the mountain now called Berry's Mountain, near Millersburg, Dauphin County. Quite substantial, it was obviously a permanent village, and the place that day was a beehive of activity. Everyone was busy preparing for the large feast. Colorful decorations were everywhere, including those draped over a large wigwam that stood in the center of the encampment. It appeared to house something of value since it was guarded by several battle-hardened warriors wielding large tomahawks.

The brothers had been caught up in the gaiety of the moment but were disappointed that they had not yet seen the bride-to-be. Then they heard a woman's voice coming from the wigwam. To their surprise, she was singing in English, and from her words they realized she must have seen them enter the camp.

The lyrics of her song were not words of joy, but a lament; a story that she was trying to convey to them. As they listened more intently, they learned that she was an English woman who had been captured and adopted by the tribe. Now she was being forced to marry the chief's son, who she did not love. She continued to sing her sad chronicle until the chief arrived with his son. At that moment, the Wingans brothers resolved to rescue this damsel in distress before the wedding ceremony could take place that very evening. They knew the guards could not understand English, and so they would have no suspicions as to what the brothers might be planning.

As the day wore on, the siblings decided on a daring plan and managed to convey their intentions to the maiden in the wigwam. They also encouraged all the guests at the forthcoming wedding to drink to excess, and by the time the celebration began it had turned into a drunken revelry. The young maiden had refrained from drinking, and so when she was given a signal by one of the brothers, she slipped out of the wigwam.

Young lovers posing on top of Love Rock (from an old photo).

Brother Harold had mounted the chief's horse, which he knew was tethered nearby, and rode up to the maiden, who jumped onto the horse and was cradled in the arms of its rider. The horse and its two riders, amid the howls of the Indians, galloped swiftly into the surrounding forest. Then, before the drunken revelers could find their horses and begin a pursuit, Harold brought the horse to a sudden stop at the place he knew his brother William would be hiding.

"Quick, take her!" shouted Harold to his twin. "Follow the path up the mountain and keep on it until you are on the other side. I will take the road below and decoy them. See!" Harold held up a blanket folded into human form, and then he and William traded places. William then galloped off with the intended bride and Harold, cradling the blanket in his arms, walked onto the lower roadway so his pursuers could see him.

The ruse gave William enough time to reach a clearing near the top of the mountain, but the Indians had seen him also. His horse was tiring under the weight of two riders, and William was soon caged in. Without anywhere else to go, he urged the horse onward until the trail ended abruptly at the edge of a cliff. It was at that exact moment that William heard Harold's voice coming from the foot of the cliff below. "Jump the horse over, and keep well on him; they have wounded me to death."

Without a moment to lose, Willliam spurred the horse over the edge of the precipice. The horse and riders landed with such force that the fall killed the horse, but both riders were thrown clear. They managed to evade the pursuing Indians and met a party of settlers the next morning.

It would be a happy ending except for the fact that the chief's son really loved the maiden, and subsequently led many search parties, hoping to find her. As months, then years, went by, he began frequenting the cliffside where his sweetheart and William Wingans made their escape.

His behavior became more erratic, and he would return to the Indian camp after his cliffside visits festooned with colorful flowers while singing and dancing wildly. His father became feebly ill and, unable to look upon his hopelessly deranged, noble son, died with a broken heart.

The tribe eventually moved away, but the mad warrior chose to remain. For five years he lived and labored at the cliff face, spending that time carving two large recesses out of the solid rock. When finished, the jilted lover,

View of Rattling Creek flowing below Lover Rock (from an old postcard).

now completely insane, sat down in one of the carved-out depressions, determined to wait there until his lover returned.

In the intervening years, William Wingans married the rescued maiden, and ten years later brought his wife back to the cliff to visit the place where they had somehow made such a miraculous escape. They made their way to the top of the precipice and walked over to its edge. Looking down they were surprised to see the jilted lover sitting in a pocket of the cliff face. He looked up at them, and when he saw the maiden he gestured to her, beckoning her to come and sit beside him in the other pocket he had carved into the cliff. With that final effort, he leaned back, and, with a peaceful smile on his face, passed into the Indians' Happy Hunting Ground; that land of eternal love and peace where he would one day be reunited with his sweetheart.

To this day a large rock at the top of the cliff where this tragic love story is said to have occurred is called "Love Rock." Its narrative has endured for centuries, as have the two side-by-side pockets in the rock face, supposedly carved there by the heart-broken warrior who, according to the legend, never gave up on his hope for regaining a lost love. He was in that sense a believer in the oft-repeated axiom that "Love is Eternal."[2]

---

2. Author unknown, *The Lykens Register*, Lykens Valley, Pennsylvania, September 1, 1898. This newspaper article is perhaps the first time the story appeared in print.

LOCATION: Along Glen Park Road near Lykens, Dauphin County, Pa

DD GPS COORDINATES: 40.56673, -76.700522

DRIVING DIRECTIONS: From Harrisburg, take Route 22 West toward Dauphin. At Dauphin take PA 225 North (Peters Mountain Road). In 7 miles turn right onto PA 325 (Clarks Valley Road). In 10 miles take a left onto Carsonville Road. In 3 miles turn right onto Back Road. In one-half mile turn left onto White Oak Road. In one-half mile turn right onto Powells Valley Road. Follow this road into Lykens, and in Lykens take a left (opposite Market Street on the right) onto Glen Park Road. An immediate left onto Parkview Road and then a right onto Love Rock Road in one-tenth mile takes you to the trailhead.

NOTE: I have been unable to find any historical references that support the contention that there is a historical basis for the Love Rock legend. Specifically, there are no references to any Wingans, in Sipe's *Indian Wars of Pennsylvania* or in his *Indian Chiefs of Pennsylvania*. Likewise, there are no Wingans mentioned in William Hunter's *Forts on the Pennsylvania Frontier*, in J. Pritts' *Mirror of Olden Time Border Life*, nor in any of the three volumes of Luther Kelker's *History of Dauphin County Pennsylvania*. Queries about the Wingans to the Lykens/Wilkens Valley Historical Society went unanswered.

CHAPTER 4

INDIAN CHIEF ROCK

The valley of Morrison's Cove extends northward from Evitts Mountain, near the village of New Enterprise in Bedford County, to the Frankstown Branch of the Juniata River at Williamsburg, Blair County. Bounded on the eastern side by Tussey Mountain and on the western edge by a chain of the Lock Mountains, its ten-to-fifteen-mile width is landlocked except for three gaps in the mountains that hem it in. In the south there is Loysburg Gap, McKee Gap affords an escape in the west, and the third is at Williamsburg to the north.

It is a matter of some speculation as to how the Valley got its name. There is no record of an earliest settler of that name. Others say it may have been of a more disreputable genesis. According to them, there was once a notorious horse-thief named Morris who plied his illegal trade throughout the eastern counties of the state. Sometimes, when the authorities got too hot on his trail, he would bring his stolen horses to a hidden sanctuary in the cove. Here he would keep them tucked safely away until he could recover them and sell them to obtain his ill-gotten gains.[1]

That explanation for the valley's title would undoubtedly not have set well with its earliest settlers if it were true. The fertile region was settled by Godfearing Swiss, German, and Scotch-Irish pioneers who believed that the Holy Word should be their only guiding light. Their other guiding principle was their strong work ethic or "earning your bread by the sweat of your brow." They believed in that old adage, "a day's work for a day's

---

1. Revered C. W. Karns, *Historical Sketches of Morrison's Cove*, 7.

View of Indian Rock along the Juniata near Williamsburg (from an old postcard).

pay" and also believed that "honesty is the best policy." Their Holy Trinity, therefore, was the axe, the Bible, and the rifle.[2]

The axe was their means of creating shelter for their families, and to clear the ground so they could plant crops to feed them. Therefore, the incessant daily chopping sounds of those ax handlers at work echoed throughout the primeval forest that surrounded them and along the Frankstown Branch of the Juniata River. Ancient forest monarchs were felled in this way and then notched so perfectly that when fitted together they formed a cozy log cabin once a stone fireplace was added, and a roaring fire was blazing in the hearth.

The fireside would have been a warm place to sit and read during the long winter months, but in almost all cases the only book to be found in any of those homesteads would have been the Bible. It governed their lives, and they feared God's retribution more than the uncertainty of their everyday existence. The Bible was their moral compass, and they believed in it implicitly. Although the Bible gave them the comfort they needed to persevere in their independent ways, the rifle was another source of comfort as well.

It was the rifle that allowed them to procure the wild game they needed to survive. It also protected them from the wild beasts of prey that roamed

2. Ibid, 3.

that same valley. Nightly screams of mountain lions and howls of wolf packs would have been intolerable except for the knowledge that their rifles would keep them safe. As time went by, their rifles would provide even more security as the era of border warfare between colonials and Native Americans dawned over the dark and quiet forest of the frontier.

It was a dark and terrible time for the colonists, and it lasted over a decade. As one historian put it in describing the ordeal, "The settlers of the mountain valleys of Huntingdon, Blair and Bedford Counties suffered terribly at the hands of the Indian allies of the British."[3] That time of trial began in 1777 with the murder of the Tully family near Fort Bedford. This was followed by more murders in Bedford County that fall. Then in November 1777, Thomas Smith and George Woods, residents of Bedford, in a letter to Pennsylvania President Thomas Wharton, described the terrible circumstances in what is now Bedford and Blair Counties.

"The present condition of this County is so truly deplorable that we should be inexcusable if we delayed a moment in acquainting you with it; an Indian war is now raging around us in the utmost fury."[4]

The ravages continued into 1778 when pioneer settler Samuel Moore and his family of seven sons and two daughters were driven out of Scotch Valley of Blair County. They had gone out searching for their stray horses and were ambushed by a large contingent of warriors.[5]

This was followed by the murder of John Guilford near present-day Altoona, Blair County, in that same year, followed by many more. Finally, in May of 1778, the Pennsylvania Assembly wrote to the Continental Congress that "upwards of thirty people had recently been killed by Indians in the present counties of Bedford, Blair, and Huntingdon."[6]

The situation only got worse after the Wyoming Massacre on July 3, 1778, which led to more murderous raids on frontier settlements by emboldened warriors. The fear those raids engendered swept over the frontier like an unstoppable fire, and the mass exodus that followed became known as The Great Runaway. It would not be until 1779 that those exiled settlers felt safe enough to return to their abandoned cabins and barns.

In the summer of that year General John Sullivan and his 5,000 troops, at the request of General George Washington, effected a terrible

---

3. C. Hale Sipe, *The Indian Wars of Pennsylvania*, 623.
4. Ibid, 526.
5. Ibid, 537.
6. Ibid, 538.

retribution upon the invaders for siding with the British and for their devastating attacks on the American frontier. Sullivan's colonial force raided the Iroquois country in Northern Pennsylvania and Southern New York, destroying many villages, burning crops, leveling their orchards, and killing their horses.

The winter following was one of the worst in the history of the United States up to that time. Rivers and lakes froze solid, and heavy snows accumulated to a depth of four feet in the mountains of New York and Pennsylvania. That wintertime became known as "the winter of the deep snow," and it could not have come at a worse time for the Iroquois. With their food supplies destroyed by Sullivan's army, many of them froze and starved to death.[7]

It was thought that after such decimation of the Iroquois Confederacy their power would be broken. Nonetheless, more atrocities and battles were to come, with one of the most disheartening for frontier families being the murder of the Bedford Scouts on the third of June 1781.

There had been reports that a Seneca raiding party had attacked several farms in what was then called the Frankstown District near Holliday's Fort, located close to present-day Hollidaysburg, Blair County. The raiders were said to have killed the farmers and taken their families prisoner. These were typical tactics that were encouraged by the British so that their Indian allies would destroy frontier settlements and create fear and panic. However, their real objective was to draw out colonial forces from behind their fortifications, thereby increasing the probability that the raiding parties would capture an officer. A captured officer could then be traded for a British officer being held captive by the colonials.

At that time this area was still part of Bedford County and would not become part of Blair County until 1846. This section was referred to as the Frankstown District, named after Indian trader Stephen Franks, who established a trading post near the aborigine village of Assunepachla. The modern-day village of Frankstown sits there today.

Shortly after the news of the Indian attacks was received, another report came to Holliday's fort claiming that the raiders' abandoned camp had been discovered near Hart's Log (now Alexandria, Huntingdon County).

---

7. Ibid, 606.

Within days, a group of forty-four men gathered at Fort Fetter (close to present-day Duncansville, Blair County) to search for the raiders. On the morning of June 3, they departed, under the command of Captain John Boyd. Boyd's force was composed of some militia volunteers, but the rest were men authorized by the Pennsylvania legislature as the Bedford County Rangers.

It was a foggy morning that June day; and hiding in that dense mist within several hundred yards of the fort was a force of Seneca Indians and a platoon of British Regulars. Boyd's men had not anticipated that the enemy would dare to come so close to the fort. Consequently, they were taken totally by surprise when the stillness of the morning was broken by war whoops and gunfire.

The struggle was short, and Boyd's force was overwhelmed. Some survivors managed to retreat back to the safety of the fort, but twelve dead men and six wounded remained on the battlefield. A rescue force of volunteers from Fort Fetter, Fort Holliday, and Fort Frankstown went to the scene of the ambush the next day. Once there they buried the dead. The rangers' defeat was not a total loss, however, since the Senecas and their British allies subsequently decided to withdraw from the area. The Bedford Rangers were eventually disbanded two years later when hostilities ended.[8]

The news of the murder of the Bedford Scouts, as they were later referred to, no doubt spread quickly over the frontier and must have caused much consternation wherever it was heard. That it did so is documented in a letter written by George Ashman, the Bedford County Lieutenant, to Joseph Reed, President of the Supreme Executive Council of Pennsylvania, dated June 12, 1781. In that missive (spelled as written) Ashman states that, as a result of the Bedford Scouts disaster,

> This County at this time is in a Deplorable situation a number of Familys are flying a way daily ever since the late damage was dun, I can assure your Excellency that if Immediate assistance is not sent to this County that the whole of the frontier Inhabitants will move off in a few days.[9]

---

8. Jim Lowe, "What's That Rock There For?" *The History Lowdown*, April 15, 2023. https://jimlowe.substack.com/p/whats-that-rock-there-for.
9. Waterman and Watkins, *History of Bedford, Somerset and Fulton Counties, Pennsylvania*, 95.

Monument to the Bedford Scouts. Located along Route 764 in Blair County, its attached plaque lists the names of the Bedford County Rangers who were killed, wounded, or taken prisoner on a foggy June 3 morning, 1781, in an ambush, later referred to as "the Battle of Frankstown," by a force of Seneca Indians and a platoon of British Regulars, near Fort Fetter (close to present-day Duncansville, Blair County).

That heightened level of anxiety might have also been fueled by the memory of a similar massacre that had occurred just the previous year near the village of Williamsburg in Woodbury Township of Morrison's Cove Valley. Described as a "most alarming stroke" in a letter dated 06 August 1780, sent to Joseph Reed (then-President of the Supreme Executive Council of Pennsylvania), John Piper, reported (spelled as written):

> Capt Phillips, an Experienced good woods man Had Engaged a Company of Rangers for the space of two Month for the Defence of Our fronteers, was Surprised at His post on Sunday, the 16 July, when the Capt., with Eleven of His Company, were all taken and Killd. When I Recevd the Intelligence, which was the day following, I marched with only ten Men directly to the Place, where we found the House Burnt to Ashes, with sundry Indian

Monument to the Phillips Rangers. Historian C. Hale Sipe said it best at the monument dedication ceremonies. "Here in the heart of the mountains of the land they loved, these rangers sleep the last long sleep, with the rocks of the mountains to guard their rest, with the murmuring winds among the trees to sound their dirge, and with the wild flowers of the mountains to utter their eulogy in the oratory of the perfumed silence. Peace to their ashes."

Tomahawks that had been lost in the Action, But found no Person Killd at that Place. But upon taking the Indian tracks, within about one Half mile we found ten of Capt. Phillip's Company with their Hands tyd and Murdered in the most Cruel Manner. "This Bold Enterprise so Alarmed the Inhabitants that our whole fronteers were upon the point of Giveing way.[10]

Living a few miles above the town of Williamsburg, Morrison's Cove, in the summer of that infamous year of 1780, Colonel John Piper appointed William Phillips as a ranger captain. He was to recruit a company of rangers whose duty was to protect valley settlements from Indian incursions. Phillips did not have much success. It was harvesttime and most men wanted to harvest their crops instead of wandering off into the mountains to scout for war parties. Nonetheless, Phillips managed to collect ten men along with his son Isaac.

10. Ibid, 94.

Having heard reports that evidence of several hostile Indian war parties had been found in both Morrison's Cove and over in neighboring Woodcock Valley, Captain Phillips felt it was his duty was to provide protection for settlers in both places. So, on the morning of July 15, 1780, he and his eleven rangers searched through the Cove and then trekked over Tussey Mountain and down into Woodcock.

There they found that the settlers had fled, leaving deserted homesteads and farms behind. After an all-day search they arrived at another deserted homestead which proved to be that of Frederick Hester. It was later learned that Hester had taken his family and fled to safety elsewhere. However, the deserted homestead seemed like a perfect refuge to Phillips since it was constructed as a blockhouse.

Hester's log home was like other pioneer homes of this area at that time, since it had been built to serve as a refuge from attacks of hostile war parties. As such, there were loopholes in the walls which allowed defenders to train musket fire on attackers. Here, in Hester's Blockhouse, Phillips decided to spend the night to give his men a much-needed rest in relative safety. They had found no evidence of hostile war parties the entire day and, as Phillips hoped, the night passed without interruption.

However, as breakfast was being prepared the next morning, one of the rangers looked out the door and realized that the cabin was surrounded by Indians. The rangers soon realized they were hopelessly outnumbered. There were at least fifty warriors, with two whites war-painted and dressed like them. The rangers decided to let the war party make the first move and awaited an attack that they knew had to be coming.

Ten of the attackers carried rifles, and the rest had bows and arrows. After some little time, sporadic gunfire was exchanged. In this crossfire, two warriors were killed and two wounded, with no casualties incurred by the rangers. These exchanges continued until mid-afternoon, when one of the chiefs was wounded. The chief's death infuriated his tribesmen, who then intensified their firing. The hail of bullets and arrows became so intense that one arrow, shot by an expert Indian archer, spiked the muzzle of a musket protruding from a musket port. It was so forcefully driven into the musket barrel that Captain Phillips would later recall that "it required the efforts of four men to withdraw the weapon."

View of Arch Rock. An amazing natural wonder located just off Route 322 at the village of the same name near Mifflintown in the Juniata River Valley of Juniata County.

Closer view of Arch Rock and Horning Run which flows into it.

Rainbow Rocks. My name for this unusual formation on a rock face along Route 322 near the Arch Rock exit in Juniata County.

Realizing that the rangers were not going to come out, the Indians set fire to the cabin. As the flames raged higher and higher, the rangers had no choice but to surrender, knowing that they most likely also faced death by doing so. After being forced to lay down their weapons, the rangers' hands were tied behind their backs. Shortly afterwards they were told that they would be marched to the large Indian village of Kittanning in the west. They had not traveled far until a halt was ordered. Five or six Indians took charge of Captain Phillips and his son and then forced them on the way again. The other rangers were left behind with their captors.

The fate of Captain Phillips' Rangers was a gruesome one. The next day a rescue party found them all tied to trees with three to five arrows sticking in their bodies and their scalps torn from their heads. Their bodies were buried where they were discovered.

Captain Phillips and his son were spared a similar fate. Both were taken to Detroit, where the Indians evidently thought the British would give them a large reward for the capture of an officer. The captain and his son survived their captivity in Detroit, and both returned home to Williamsburg at the close of the Revolutionary War. It is recorded that the fate of his rangers preyed heavily upon the mind of the captain until his dying days. He is buried in a small country cemetery two miles south of Williamsburg.[11]

A small monument marking the final resting place of his rangers was erected along Route 26 on Tussey Mountain near Saxton in Woodcock Valley, Bedford County. Likewise, there is a monument along Route 764 near Hollidaysburg, Bedford County, that is dedicated to the memory of the Bedford Scouts who died in the Battle of Frankstown on June 3, 1781. Both monuments are reminders of the colonials who fought and died in the many battles with Native Americans that occurred throughout the tri-county area of Bedford, Huntingdon, and Blair Counties during the days of border warfare. The only thing missing, however, is any kind of memorial to the Indians who fought in those same wars Nonetheless, it seems that Mother Nature had a final say about that.

That there is a mountain landmark called Indian Chief Rock in Blair County should come as no surprise to those who have read the preceding paragraphs and now know the county's colonial history. As the reader has seen, there are many stirring accounts of the bloody battles that took place around this area in that earlier day. And it is perhaps that history that may have prompted someone to bestow that name on this odd rock pinnacle that sits along the Raystown Branch of the Juniata River near Williamsburg in Blair County.

The local history buff who named the rock was obviously aware of the area's many battles between settlers and Native Americans and also must have known about the monuments erected to honor the colonials who died in those struggles. They therefore perhaps decided that the Indians needed a monument to honor their dead as well. Although it must have required a lot of imagination to think of it as such (and still does for that matter), Indian Chief Rock was so named, it is recalled, because it reminded the person who named it of an erect Indian chief wearing a war bonnet headdress. Regardless of the reason behind the name, it still serves as a fitting memorial to the many Indians who died in a desperate and complicated struggle to save their land.

---

11. Details on the murder of Captain Phillips' Rangers were taken from an address delivered by C. Hale Sipe, upon the occasion of the reinterment of the bones of the victims at the new memorial site, on May 28, 1933.

ANOTHER INTERESTING LANDMARK ALONG THE JUNIATA

There is yet another rocky reminder of the Native Americans who once lived along the waters of the Juniata River, and it's not that far from Indian Chief Rock. This one is known locally as Indian Face Rock, and it supposedly has a Native American connection too. Local legends relate that this was once a favorite rendezvous point for several native tribes living in the area. Those same legends claim that sometime in the mid-1700s those same

A view of Indian Face Rock along the Juniata near Mifflintown as it appeared on the cover of an earlier historical pamphlet.

Same view of Indian Face Rock taken within the last ten years. It hasn't changed much over time! (photo courtesy of Sheila Yorks)

Indians carved a face into the rock. The legends do not say why they did so or how long it took them, but it seems much more likely that nature was the artist that created the face!

The picture is still there, having withstood the effects of centuries of weathering to an astonishing degree. I have included a photo of the face as it looked decades ago and another showing how it looks today. The likeness is quite remarkable, and it is so distinct that it is understandable how it became known as Indian Face Rock.[12]

---

12. The author is indebted to local resident Sheila Yorks for details on the legend of Indian Face Rock and for the picture of same. The original photo of the Indian Face appeared in a small booklet published fifty or sixty years ago (exact date unknown).

LOCATION:

Indian Chief Rock is a peak in the township of Catharine, Blair County, Pennsylvania, and has an elevation of 1,086 feet. Indian Chief Rock is situated nearby to the hamlet Robeson Extension and the village of Williamsburg.

Indian Face Rock is located along the Juniata River near Mifflintown, Juniata County, slightly upriver from the Pennsylvania Fish and Boat Commission boat launch at 1690 William Penn Highway.

DD GPS COORDINATES:

Indian Chief Rock: 40.473404 N -78.208851 W
Indian Face Rock: 40.551894 N, -77.374762 W

DRIVING DIRECTIONS:

Indian Chief Rock: Follow Route 45 West out of Boalsburg near State College, Centre County. Follow Route 45 through Pine Grove Mills and Water Street to a T intersection with Route 453 South. Turn left onto Route 453 South and then bear right onto Route 22 South/West. Follow Route 22 West until you can take a left onto Juniata River Road (PA-866). Follow PA-866 toward Williamsburg for three miles. Indian Chief Rock is across the river on the left. It is best seen from the Lower Trail which parallels PA-866.

CHAPTER 5

MYSTERIES OF HAWK MOUNTAIN

One of Pennsylvania's greatest natural attractions is a 2,600-acre natural area in southeastern Pennsylvania that is home to the world's first refuge for birds of prey. Hawk Mountain Sanctuary is a wild bird sanctuary that sits on Hawk Mountain, part of the Blue Mountain or Kittatinny Ridge that spans parts of Berks and Schuylkill Counties. Located along the stretch birdwatchers call the Appalachian flyway, it is a prime spot for viewing migrating raptors. Vast flocks of hawks, eagles, and falcons pass by the lookouts on the rocks during the late summer and early fall of each year, and it is not unusual to see 20,000 or more at both of those times. The Sanctuary is believed to be the oldest and largest member-supported raptor conservation organization in the world. In 1965 it was designated as a National Natural Landmark, and in 2022 it was listed on the National Register of Historic Places.[1]

Hawk Mountain is also known for its hiking trails, which are as short as half a mile or as long as twenty-one miles. The trails have varying levels of difficulty, ranging from easy to difficult, and so can accommodate hikers of all ages and conditions. Along those pathways are many overlooks, which offer gorgeous views of the surrounding countryside, especially when the fall foliage is at its peak. The South View affords one of the most spectacular panoramas, where you can see more than forty miles. Likewise, at the North View there is a 70-mile vista that takes the breath away.

---

1. Marcus Schneck, "Hawk Mountain and its 'unique history and legacy' earn it a spot on the National Register of Historic Places," published April 28, 2022, on the *PennLive* online local news platform.

Other natural attractions like the River of Rocks, and the Blue Rocks Boulder Field, lure hikers also, and so it is no wonder that the area has become known as a favorite hiking spot for outdoor adventurers. In other circles, it is also known as one of America's most haunted places. And there is good reason for that if the area's legends and oral traditions can be taken as truthful sources.[2]

Some of those accounts date back to the times when the area was a revered spot for the Lenni Lenape Indians. They were awed by the majesty of the ridge and named it Kittatinny, meaning Endless Mountain or Great Mountain.[3] This was a favorite hunting place for these aboriginal hunters, and it was here that they conducted some of their most sacred rituals, many at a ceremonial ring that once decorated the mountainside. Where that ring was located is not known today, but there have been reports of a luminous ten-foot-tall apparition which some say is the spirit of an Indian which guards the location of the ring. It is seen most often on Hawk Mountain Road, and those who have encountered it report feeling an overwhelming sense of dread caused by the evil vibrations emanating from the revenant.[4]

There is no doubt that the Lenni Lenape did not take kindly to the first Europeans who settled here. Settlers in Berks County were subjected to numerous raids by Indian war parties, especially during the times of the French and Indian War and then during the Revolutionary War. It was during the early years of the French and Indian War that one of those war parties attacked the family of Jacob Gerhardt, who was living in a log cabin he had built for his family on Hawk Mountain. The warriors slaughtered the entire family, except for one son, who managed to escape and then years later came back to build his own homestead on the site of his father's original log cabin. Reports of wails and screams heard at this site have led people to say that the ghosts of the Gerhardt family still haunt Hawk Mountain to this day.[5]

If the Gerhardts do haunt the mountain, then their spirits may have company, if the story of another mass murder is also true. In this case aboriginal warriors were not the perpetrators of the slaughter, but it was

---

2. Josh Popichak, "Hawk Mountain Hauntings, Part I: Shambacher's Tavern," online publication by *the Saucon Source, LLC*, online news publisher, October 24, 2024.
3. Doctor George P. Donehoo, *Indian Villages and Place Names in Pennsylvania*, 84-85.
4. Josh Popichak, "Hawk Mountain Hauntings, Part I: Shambacher's Tavern," online publication by *the Saucon Source, LLC*, online news publisher, October 24, 2024.
5. Ibid.

Some of the unusual rocks to be found on Hawk Mountain (photo courtesy of Clifford Zeller).

instead the work of one man—a man of German descent who was perhaps the one and only serial killer who ever lived on Hawk Mountain.

In 1850 Matthias Schambacher purchased the house built by the Gerhardt's son, converting it into a tavern/rest stop for travelers heading to the north country. Not long afterwards rumors began to spread about mysterious disappearances of traveling salesmen who had stopped at the tavern for refreshment. People then noticed that Schambacher would sometimes come to town selling clothing and other items that were exactly like the goods carried by the missing salespeople. Particularly unsettling was the time when a merchant selling Civil War uniforms disappeared and a few days later Schambacher turned up selling those very same uniforms.

Stories then surfaced as to how passersby sometimes heard screams and moans coming from Schambacher's barn; and how they were sometimes chased from his property by a hatchet-wielding Schambacher in blood-stained clothes. No one could prove that the disagreeable tavernkeeper had committed any murders, but then in 1879, when on his deathbed, Schambacher made a dying confession. He said he had killed at least eleven travelers who had stopped at his inn and had disposed of the bodies by burying parts in the woods for the animals to get rid of and by throwing some down a well. Later owners of the building corroborated Schambacher's claims when they uncovered human remains buried along a hedgerow behind the house and found skeletons in all three of the wells on the property.[6]

Over the years Schambacher's infamy did not die, with his reputation as a serial killer becoming firmly entrenched as part of the oral traditions of the region. Reports of phantom lights seen on the mountain and ethereal voices that seem to whisper from the dark woods surrounding the Schambacher tavern, which still stands on its original site, have only cemented the area's reputation as a haunted and mysterious place. But there is one more lingering mystery here that is not as renowned as the aforementioned ones, the unsolved murder of the hermit of Hawk Mountain.

Embellished accounts of this crime can be found on various websites, but I have found what is probably the earliest and most authentic version, in a 1949 newspaper article published in Lancaster. The article published September 15, 1949, in *The Pennsylvania Dutchman*, makes for interesting reading, since much of this now defunct newspaper was in the Pennsylvania Dutch dialect, with many translations in English for those who did not speak the language. The newspaper eventually evolved into *Pennsylvania Folklife Magazine*.

The headline for the article was "ECHOES OF HAWK MOUNTAIN: The unfathomable mystery of Matthias Berger." Joel Hartman, the writer, begins his article as follows:

> "As I turned off the Reading Pottsville highway and headed north on Route 895, I gazed for a few moments at the Blue Mountains to my right. Majestically they rose out of the valley like a tyrannical monarch, sitting on a high throne, looking down upon his subjects. It was midsummer and the entire mountain was dressed in full splendor of bluish green hues. Only here and there did the solitary trunk of a dead pine tree rise above the green foliage to contrast sharply against a cloudless sky.
>
> "Lapping along the lower fringes of forest, the Little Schuylkill wound its way through the valley. Its waters, no longer black with silt, were now tinged with a hue of brown, evidence of a polluting anthracite industry to the north having passed its peak. Clinging close to the riverbank were the tracks of the Reading Railroad, over

---

6. Josh Popichak, "Hawk Mountain Hauntings, Part I: Shambacher's Tavern," online publication by *the Saucon Source, LLC*, online news publisher, October 24, 2024.

which have rolled millions of tons of 'black gold' on its way to feed the gigantic furnaces of American industry."

"Rolling rapidly over the hilly terrain, my car rounded a curve, and I saw before me a dozen or more housetops, the little village of Drehersville, nestled in the lower lap of the mountain.

"My car sped around another curve and the village vanished before my eyes, but in the inner recesses of my mind, another vision stirred. Since my ancestors, for several generations, had lived in this valley, I was somewhat familiar with its legends and traditions; and now, sentimentally perhaps, I began to grope back through the fog and mist of dim memories in an attempt to bring to light some of the echoes of the past. The first name to come to mind was that of Matthias Berger."[7]

Hartman then continues to tell the story of the man locals referred to as *der alt Modas* (the old style or old fashion) Berger. Berger immigrated to America sometime before 1850, settling in the "Eck" or the highlands of Berks County. On a high clearing on top of the *Sparkerbarich*, a colloquial name for present-day Hawk Mountain, Berger built a small hut. When asked why he wanted to reside in such a remote spot so high up on the mountain, the little hermit declared he wanted to be closer to his Creator.

Here, in a teepee-shaped shelter built from chestnut saplings and roofed with straw and leaves mixed with clay, Berger eked out a meager existence. He survived in this small hovel with money he earned by helping neighboring farmers and by cutting cordwood. He avoided human contact for most of his life, but being a devout Catholic, he never missed attending mass at Reading.

Returning from one of his trips to Reading one day, he discovered that a forest fire had ravaged the mountain where his hovel was located. Warned by his neighbors that his hut was now probably nothing more than ashes and that he was welcome to stay with them, Berger replied "*Gott wurde meine hutte nicht verbrennen*" (God wouldn't burn down my shanty), and much to everyone's surprise the hut had survived the blaze, except for some slight singeing of the front door.

---

7. Joel Hartman, "Echoes of Hawk Mountain," *The Pennsylvania Dutchman*, Lancaster, Pennsylvania, September 15, 1949. The author took all the details about Matthias Berger which appear in this chapter, from this article.

Although he was not averse to dealing with them, Berger considered his neighbors to be "too worldly" and so preferred his solitary lifestyle. On the other hand, he enjoyed the company of their children, often entertaining them around a large table in his arbor. Their laughter could often be heard echoing through the hilltop as they ate the lunches that they had brought with them, sharing them with their beloved *Modas*, and sipping on the hot Blue Mountain tea he would brew for them.

Despite his eccentricities, Berger was well-liked by his neighbors and respected for his deep religious convictions, which he often shared with them. They also appreciated him for the way he amused their children. It was for these reasons that it came as a complete shock to them one day when they saw vultures circling over the large boulder field at Owl's Head Rocks, and when investigating further found Berger's body sprawled across the rocks.

The morning of June 25, 1890, had started off as hot and still, with nary a breeze stirring the dried bushes and trees, all parched by lack of rain for the last three weeks. Then toward noon, a lone spring wagon could be seen on the road coming off the mountain and down into Drehersville. Thick clouds of dust rose behind it as it came rattling down the road at a high rate of speed, indicating the driver had some news of import to share with the villagers.

Harry Mohl wasted no time raising the alarm. He said he had gone up the mountain to look for bees, and while there had decided to stop and pay his respects to Berger. When he got to the clearing where Berger's home was located, he found no one there, and when he entered the old man's shelter, he was dismayed to find it in total disarray. The bed had been torn apart, the straw pillow ripped open, and straw strewn all over the floor. It looked, said Mohl, "as though a cyclone had hit it!"[8]

Concerned villagers, realizing no one had seen the old man for at least three weeks, immediately organized search parties and went up the mountain to look for the missing hermit. They tramped through the underbrush, explored dark hollows, and peered into every deep recess in the rocks, until someone exclaimed, "Here he is!"

As the searchers gathered around the body, they gazed upon a sickening sight. The body lay face down, with the pockets of its clothing turned

---

8. Ibid.

View of the Lehigh Valley from the rocks on Hawk Mountain where Matthias Berger's body was found (photo courtesy of Clifford Zeller).

inside out. It had obviously lain there for some time, most likely the entire three weeks during which no one had seen Berger. In that period, vultures had stripped the bones of their flesh, leaving nothing more than a skeleton. When the searchers turned the body over, they were greeted by a grinning skull. Hardly the countenance to be expected on a murder victim, but perhaps one fitting for a man so committed to his faith as Matthias Berger.

It was agreed that Berger had been the victim of a robbery, given the state of his hovel, and his turned-out pockets. It was also apparent that he had made every effort to affect an escape from the thieves who killed him since his body was found on the rock formation two miles from his home. He was given a decent burial in the churchyard at Reading, and for years afterwards there were many who held hopes that his killers would eventually be identified and brought to justice. Unfortunately, that never happened, and to this day the murder remains unsolved. It must be just another source of dissatisfaction for Berger's spirit, along with the fact that one of his most fervent wishes, to die in church, was never granted to him. Hopefully, those disaffections have not spoiled his life in the world to come.[9]

---

9. Ibid.

NOTE: No mention of a Gerhardt family being murdered by Indians in Berks or Schuylkill Counties was found in Sipe's *Indian Wars of Pennsylvania*, in the 1884 first edition of M. L. Montgomery's *History of Berks County*, or in Munsell's 1881 edition of the *History of Schuylkill County*. The tale therefore is of doubtful origin unless there is corroborative evidence in some other histories of the area.

LOCATION: Hawk Mountain Sanctuary is located on the Blue Mountain in Albany Township of Berks County.

DD GPS COORDINATES: 40°38'27"N 75°59'32"W

DRIVING DIRECTIONS:
From Harrisburg, take I-81 North/I-78 East, following I-78 East into Hamburg. Turn onto Route 61 North, then follow until you can turn right onto 895 North (Summer Valley Road). Follow until you can turn right onto Hawk Mountain Road into Hawk Mountain Sanctuary.

CHAPTER 6

LANDMARKS OF PENNSYLVANIA'S FRONTIER DAYS

That Pennsylvania's earliest colonial settlers lived in constant threat of attack by warring Native Americans is clear from many historical records. Accounts included in the earlier chapters in this volume and in the author's *Pennsylvania Fireside Tales* volumes and in the other volumes of this *Pennsylvania Mountain Landmarks* series make that clear as well. The native sons did not appreciate how colonial settlers were taking over their prime hunting lands by overhunting and by driving their game away as they settled in the animals' natural habitat.

They therefore attempted to drive those settlers out, using their typical style of guerrilla warfare. As such, their method was not to attack settlements with large bodies of warriors. Warring parties usually consisted of less than twenty members: sometimes even having as few as three. It was an effective strategy since smaller groups could stealthily sneak past sentries, no matter how alert or experienced they were. Those same raiding parties could then fall upon colonial settlers, murder and pillage their homes, then disappear as stealthily and quickly as they came. Like bolts of lightning from a thundering sky, they were gone long before the alarm could be spread, and chase could be given by rangers or troops.

Settlers coped as well as they could, sometimes using innovative measures to avoid disasters. One unique episode, illustrating a clever strategy used by a protective mother, was recorded in the history of the area in which her family was one of the first settlers. The incident was recalled by John Bierly, born in 1779 in Northumberland County.

He was the second son of Anthony Bierly, a veteran of the Revolutionary War, who in 1791 brought his family from Mahantango Creek, Snyder County, to a 300-acre tract in what is now Rebersburg, Brush Valley, Centre County. John was twelve years old at that time, but later in life he would say that his mother would recall to him the episodes of their earlier days in old Northumberland.

She would often relate to him, he would begin, "how she secreted him, when but a few months old, in a sugar-trough in the woods, and fled with the rest of the children while the Indians made an attack on the settlement. The Indians did not discover him, and he was found uninjured on the return of the family when the danger was over!" Mr. Bierly lived a long and productive life, dying at age 91 in 1870.[1]

Such innovative acts of courage saved the day in some cases, but settlers had no choice but to devise a more comprehensive and effective means of defense; construction of frontier fortresses. This innovation has led to some disagreements regarding just which structures should be referred to as "forts." There are those who claim that only the large bastions built by colonial troops or by militia forces specifically for military or defensive purposes should be called forts. On the other hand, others believe that this does not go far enough. They say that any of the private or public reinforced shelters built by ordinary citizens for defensive purposes during colonial times should be classified as forts also.

Ordinary citizens erected blockhouses (so-called "private forts"[2]) on their properties, others fortified their farmhouses as well. Small fortresses like these would afford them some degree of protection, but it was not enough. It was a patchwork of defenses with no overall plan, with the fortified places positioned at points where it was assumed attacks would most likely come.

Attacks did continue to come, intensifying after British General Edward Braddock's disastrous defeat on July 9, 1755, at the Battle of the Monongahela. Afterwards, Cumberland County Judge (later Lieutenant Colonel in the colonial army) John Armstrong wrote a letter, dated November 2,

---
1. John Blair Linn, *History of Centre and Clinton Counties, Pennsylvania*, 179.
2. William A. Hunter, *Forts on the Pennsylvania Frontier*, 178.

1755, to the Provincial Governor, stating (sic) "I'm of opinion that no other means than a Chain of Block Houses along or near the South side of the Kittatinny Mountain, from Susquehanna to the Temporary Line, can Secure the Lives and Properties of the old Inhabitants of this county."[3]

Then on November 8 the Governor received a petition from settlers in the Paxton Narrows demanding that the Assembly would [sic] "either enact a Militia Law or grant a sufficient Sum of Money to maintain such a Number of regular Troops as may be thought necessary to defend our Frontiers and build Fortifications in proper Places."[4]

By the end of the month the heretofore peace-loving Quaker Assembly had passed both recommended measures into law. The Militia Act ("An act for the Better Ordering and Regulating Such as Are Willing and Desirous to Be United for Military Purposes within This Province") was signed by Governor Morris on November 25, with a second act for financing the Militia Act passing on the very next day.[5]

The building of forts and recruitment of troops began almost immediately in the following year. The plan was to build a chain of forts from the Susquehanna to the Delaware River, situated from ten to fifteen miles apart. The first of that chain to be built, Fort Dupui, was situated on the Delaware River in Monroe County. The next was Fort Hamilton, near present-day Stroudsburg, also in Monroe County. Forts were then built in Schuylkill, Berks, Lebanon, and Dauphin Counties, with the crowning touch later being Fort Augusta in Northumberland County. These were the principal forts east of the Susquehanna. The chain of colonial forts then continued across the Susquehanna toward the west. Forts were built in Juniata, Huntingdon, Fulton, Franklin, and Cumberland Counties with the last one completed in 1756.[6]

Each fort was supplemented by surrounding blockhouses, smaller places of defense often erected by desperate settlers at their own expense and by their own labors. The other difference between forts and blockhouses was that blockhouses were defended by those who built them, while the much-larger forts were garrisoned by a body of troops from one of the three battalions of the Pennsylvania Regiment—continental soldiers from each Pennsylvania county.[7]

---

3. Ibid.
4. Ibid, 183.
5. Ibid.
6. C. Hale Sipe, *The Indian Wars of Pennsylvania*, 252–53.
7. Ibid.

The relative proximity of forts and blockhouses afforded settlers a less haphazard safety net when murderous war parties attacked settlements. Although that safety net was strengthened by the troops garrisoned at the frontier forts, the sheer number of soldiers sometimes created resentment on the part of the settlers. The forts oftentimes were not large enough to house all the militiamen stationed there, and many of them were sometimes billeted at local farms, often at the displeasure of the farmer.

With small homes that were not commodious enough for guests, the farmers felt exploited and crowded. Colonel Conrad Weiser received a complaint to that effect in a letter dated June 24, 1756, from Captain Busse of Fort Northkill, located near present-day Shartlesville in Berks County. Busse indicated that: "The people are not at all pleased that some 40 men are kept at the Fort at Northkill, since only 20 can stay at the fort and the others at Lang's and Kanter's."[8]

Life inside the forts could also be uncomfortable for settlers who fled to them to escape aboriginal war parties. Crowded inside, sometimes for weeks at a time, frightened colonists must have felt tense and claustrophobic. They also undoubtedly tired quickly of the spartan lifestyle imposed upon them. Various historical accounts provide a picture of what living inside a fort was really like.

Accounts from sources like Withers' *Chronicles of Border Warfare*, Pritts' *Mirror of Olden Time Border Life*, and Loudon's *Indian Narratives*, indicate that frontier fort amenities were scarce and living conditions therein were rudimentary. Living was communal, with families forced to live in close proximity. Limited space within the fort's walls meant barracks and kitchens had to be shared with complete strangers. That limited space also meant less than desirable sanitation facilities and limited access to fresh food grown in family plots.

Besides the lack of personal comforts, residents would also be commandeered to maintain the fort structures, farm small plots within the fort walls, and gather supplies for the sustenance of all. The result was that their social life was severely curtailed since leisure activities were limited.

The combination of all those undesirable environmental factors was overwhelming enough, but the ever-present threat of an Indian attack heightened the degree of stress to what to some must have seemed an intolerable level. Although residents undoubtedly felt stressed over the

---
8. William A. Hunter, *Forts on the Pennsylvania Frontier*, 317.

possibility of such an attack and their inability to tend to their own farms, soldiers in the fort must have been even more anxious about such confinement since it was up to them to defend the fort. Consequently, they had to be constantly vigilant day and night, taking shifts to always be on guard.

The combination of strong fortifications and plentiful troop numbers usually meant Indian attacks could be thwarted, but sometimes the war parties succeeded in burning a fort and in capturing/killing its inhabitants. Then, as the era of Native American warfare passed, those forts that did survive were often not maintained and so left to the ravages of the elements. On the other hand, practical locals, seeing the logs going to waste, would carry them off to build their own homes.

As a result, most of the wooden structures gradually disappeared, with only their foundations left to give evidence of where they once proudly stood. However, some of the smaller private wooden blockhouses and those made of stone did survive, and it is a few of those interesting landmarks that we want to discuss in a chapter of their own. Before introducing those last survivors, however, it is also interesting to note that replicas of some of the colonial frontier forts have been created by dedicated historians. Following are some notes on nine of the most striking that the author deems as must-see places worthy of a visit.

FORT NECESSITY

An impressive reconstruction of this fort near Farmington in Fayette County gives the visitor an appreciation for the look and feel of the circular palisaded fort George Washington's Virginia Regiment hastily constructed to defend themselves from a large force of French and Indians advancing from Fort Duquesne in 1754. In a pouring rain on the morning of July 3, the battle of the Great Meadows began, but the outnumbered Washington was forced to surrender that same night, and the French took possession of the makeshift fort, burning it before returning to Fort Duquesne.

Today that battle, in the summer of 1754 at the stronghold Washington dubbed Fort Necessity, is regarded as the opening salvo in the struggle that has become known to history as the French and Indian War. The site is preserved as Fort Necessity National Battlefield and is currently administered by the National Park Service.

Fort Necessity Reconstruction. Located near Farmington in Fayette County, the original palisaded fort was hastily constructed by George Washington's Virginia Regiment to defend themselves from a large force of French and Indians, but in the ensuing "Battle of the Great Meadows", the outnumbered colonials were forced to surrender and the French took possession of the makeshift fort and burned it to the ground.

FORT ROBERDEAU

A similar historic site can be found in Tyrone Township just outside Altoona in Blair County. Fort Roberdeau was erected in 1778, during the American Revolution, at the direction of General Daniel Roberdeau to protect those working in nearby lead mining and smelting operations. Those efforts were critical to provide lead musket balls and cannon balls to colonial troops. Moreover, protections were important because the work was being done amidst a nest of Tories and their Indian allies. The fort therefore also served as a haven for soldiers and settlers traveling through the region.

Along with its sturdy horizontal log walls with a bastion at each corner, there were also an officers' quarters, a powder magazine and other necessary structures. Reconstruction of the fort began in 1939 and was not finally completed until the 1976 bicentennial year. It was added to the National Register of Historic Places in 1974.

Fort Roberdeau Reconstruction. Built to defend workers mining lead from nearby mines, this Blair County landmark was named in honor of General Daniel Roberdeau but was popularly known as the "Lead Mine Fort".

Fort Ligonier Reconstruction. A Westmoreland County fort that was never conquered. Serving as a valuable staging area for British troops during the French and Indian War, it was attacked twice by Native Americans and their French allies but withstood those assaults.

FORT LIGONIER

Another notable reconstruction of a frontier fort can be found in the town that grew up around it in Westmoreland County. Fort Ligonier, built upon a high bluff overlooking Loyalhanna Creek, was a formidable British fortress. Its moat, mortars, canons, howitzers, and "Friesian Horses" (pointed wooden obstacles with sharpened fraises, sometimes shod with iron, which were used to block entrances or to close gaps in the fort's walls), proved to be an effective defensive barrier during the French and Indian War.

All of those defensive weapons and constructions can be seen there today, and so it is heralded on the Fort Ligonier website as the finest reconstructed fortification from the French and Indian War. Adding to its laurels is the fact that it was never taken by an enemy. The fort served as a valuable staging area for British troops during the French and Indian War, and although attacked twice by Native Americans and their French allies, it withstood those assaults, and no subsequent attempts were made to breech its walls. It was decommissioned from active service in 1766. Preservation efforts began in 1934 and are ongoing yet today.

FORT HANNA'S TOWN

Westmoreland County can boast of yet one more extensive reproduction of a frontier fort from the colonial period. This small fortress was built in 1773 when Virginia claimed ownership of what later became part of Pennsylvania. It was during that year that a conflict arose between the Colony of Virginia and the Shawnee and Mingo Indians who also claimed the land. A small stockade fort, made of pointed logs set upright surrounding a blockhouse and a spring, was built here to protect travelers and settlers from expected Indian attacks. During the American Revolution, the fort became important as a recruitment center, a supply depot, and housing for colonial troops.

The bastion was initially named Fort Reed, but as a community grew up around it, the community and the fort adopted the name Hanna's Town in honor of Robert Hanna who had set up a travelers' inn here sometime before the start of the Revolutionary War. It was in Hanna's Tavern that the first English court west of the Alleghenies was established. The town also became the first county seat of Westmoreland County until an

Fort Hannastown Reconstruction. Another Westmoreland County stockaded fort made of pointed logs set upright surrounding a blockhouse and a spring. It was built here to protect travelers and settlers from expected Indian attacks. During the American Revolution, the fort became important as a recruitment center, a supply depot, and housing for colonial troops.

overwhelming force of 100 Seneca warriors, under the command of their great war chief Guyasuta, and about 60 Canadian rangers attacked the town, burning it to the ground. Historians have called that same attack "the hardest blow inflicted by savages during the Revolution within the limits of the Western Pennsylvania settlements."[9]

The fort and its defenders, many of whom were good marksmen, managed to hold off the attackers, killing at least two and wounding several more. The attackers chose not to continue the attack the next morning, as parties of armed horsemen from the surrounding area began to arrive. Only one person inside the stockade was wounded during the siege. Margaret Shaw was shot in the breast when trying to rescue a small child which had toddled into danger. She died from her wound two weeks later. See the chapter titled "Hell Hath No Fury" in the author's *Pennsylvania Fireside Tales Volume 8* for Margaret Shaw's sad story and for more details on the burning of Hanna's Town.

---

9. Nathan Zipfel, *Westmoreland County Genealogical Project*, Chapter XXVI "The Destruction of Hannastown," found at www.pa-roots.com/westmoreland/.

Entrance Gate to Fort Hannastown. Attacked and burned on July 13, 1782, by a raiding party of Indians and their British allies, the fort was never rebuilt, but the sad story of Peggy Shaw's heroic rescue of an infant child at the gate during that siege still lives on in the annals of Westmoreland County history.

The town was never rebuilt, and its scorched ground was later converted to farmland. In 1969, the Westmoreland County Historical Society identified the original site of the fort and commenced a reconstruction project. Their efforts have resulted in the replication of several town buildings, the Hanna Tavern/Courthouse, three vintage late 18th century log houses, the reconstructed fort, blockhouse, and a wagon shed. The site is maintained and operated by the Westmoreland County Historical Society and the Westmoreland County Parks and Recreation Department.

FORT BEDFORD

Although its exact site has been lost to history, this fort was another British bastion constructed during the French and Indian War. Completed in 1758, its sturdy walls of upright logs and five bastions, surrounded by the Juniata River and a dry moat that was nine feet deep and ten feet wide at the bottom, made it a formidable deterrent to British adversaries. The British were so assured of the fort's defenses, in fact, that they considered it to be impregnable. They were so confident that this was the case that they used it as a supply post in their western campaigns, particularly that of General John Forbes. Historians would later refer to it as the "Grand Central Station of the Forbes campaign."[10]

The fort was never attacked directly by Indians, but during the Revolutionary War it was manned by Bedford County militia to protect settlers from Native American marauders. It was near here in 1769 that James Smith and fifty of his famous "Black Boys" ambushed a contingent of eighty pack horses belonging to Indian traders that they thought were destined to be delivered to their Indian enemies and which they were sure included "warlike stores."[11]

The bushwhackers were determined to prevent that at all costs. They had been subjected to so many warrior raids that to them, supplying those warriors with more war materials would be "a kind of murder at the expense of the blood and treasure of the frontier."[12] They accordingly decided to take matters into their own hands and so ten of them concealed themselves alongside the road the pack train would take.

Those Scotch-Irish frontiersmen, with blackened faces to better camouflage themselves and to resemble Indians on the warpath, were "crack shots." As the pack train got within range, the riflemen aimed and fired, the roar of their muskets echoing through the Juniata Narrows and across Warrior Ridge and Sideling Hill.

Their unerring aim was deadly. Almost all the pack horses were killed, their handlers fled for their lives, and the victors burned all the spoils that had fallen with the horses, including rum, lead, scalping knives, and tomahawks. This pre-Revolutionary War event was a criminal act, a direct affront to his majesty the king, and so a party of Highland soldiers from Fort Loudon took some prisoners merely on suspicion of guilt.

There were subsequent clashes between the King's forces at Fort Loudon and the frontiersmen before peace was restored. It was a remarkable series of events, and ones which some historians consider as the first steps toward the American Revolution. It has also been regaled as such in a movie and in a novel titled *Allegheny Uprising*. (See the chapter titled "Bloody Run" in the author's *Pennsylvania Fireside Tales Volume 2* for complete details of that important event)

---

10. https://www.legendsofamerica.com/pa-fortbedford/.
11. Colonel James Smith, *An Account of the Remarkable Occurrences in the Life and Travels of Colonel James Smith*, 108 ff.
12. Ibid.

Following the end of the Revolutionary War, troubles with the Indians declined, and Fort Bedford was eventually abandoned and razed. In honor of its 200th anniversary, the fort's log blockhouse was reconstructed, and is currently used as a museum operated under the auspices of Bedford County.

FORT LOUDON

Named after John Campbell, 4th Earl of Loudoun and Governor General of Virginia, this was yet another British fort in colonial Pennsylvania. It was built in 1756 during the French and Indian War by the Second Battalion of the Pennsylvania Regiment commanded by Colonel John Armstrong.

Construction began in November after a site was selected near Parnell Knob on land owned by farmer Matthew Patton. Patton had just started building his farmhouse here, so Armstrong, much to the chagrin of the enterprising farmer, incorporated it into the construction plan of the fort. It followed the standard design for the frontier forts of the day: typically, a 100-foot square stockade with a bastion at each of the four corners. Inside

Fort Loudon Reconstruction. This Franklin County fort was an important post throughout the colonial wars, but it became infamous when in 1765 it was assaulted by James Smith and other angry settlers, demanding their guns, which had been confiscated after they destroyed supplies intended for Native American raiders.

were a barracks, officers' quarters, a gunpowder magazine, a kitchen, and a storehouse.

Additional defensive works included outer triangular mounds called ravelins below each bastion. Surrounding all outside walls of the fort was a sloping bank, called a glacis, to make an assault even more difficult. Although it must have looked impressive, there was one individual who thought otherwise.

The Reverend Thomas Barton, an army chaplain who was stationed at Fort Loudoun (as it was then spelled), denigrated it in a letter dated July 21, 1758: "The Fort is a poor Piece of Work, irregularly built, & badly situated at the Bottom of a Hill Subject to Damps & noxious Vapours. It has something like Bastions supported by Props, which if an Enemy should cut away, down tumbles Men & all . . . The Fort is properly a square Ridout of 120 feet."[13]

The fortress was an important post throughout the colonial wars, but it became infamous when in 1765 it was assaulted by James Smith and other angry settlers, demanding their guns, which had been confiscated after

One of Fort Loudon's Bastions with its swivel gun. With simialr bastions at all four corners, the fortress was a welcome place of refuge for Franklin County settlers during the times of the colonial wars.

---

13. William A. Hunter, "Fort Loudon Revisited," *Cumberland County History,* Volume 12, no. 1, Summer 1995, 3–12.

Closeup of one of Fort Loudon's Bastions and its swivel gun. The iron or brass swivel gun was highly effective in defending frontier forts against close range attacks throughout the American colonial period and the Revolutionary war.

Closeup of Fort Loudon's Pallisades. The tightly-fitted upright logs forming the outer walls of the fort provided adequate protection from enemy arrows and musket balls.

they destroyed supplies intended for Native Americans (see Fort Bedford on preceding pages).

The garrison, low on powder and ammunition, retreated to Fort Bedford. It was never garrisoned again and was used only for storage, until 1767 when Matthew Patton demolished it and rebuilt his farmhouse, using some of the lumber for his new home.[14] A replica of this Franklin County fort was built in 1993, through dedicated efforts of the Fort Loudon Historical Society, which maintains and administers the impressive site today.

FORT AUGUSTA

This Northumberland County stronghold in the upper Susquehanna Valley was the military headquarters of American forces from the time of the French and Indian War to the end of the Revolutionary War. Built near (not on) the present-day town of Shamokin, on the site of the largest Indian town in Pennsylvania, Shamokin was the headquarters of Oneida chief Shikellamy (see the chapter titled "Blue Hill" in the author's *Pennsylvania Mountain Landmarks Volume 2*, and the chapter titled "Faces From

Model of Fort Augusta at the original site of the colonial fort, which was so formidable that it was never attacked. It Stands in front of the Hunter House, home of the Northumberland Historical Society, at Sunbury, Northumberland County.

---

14. Ibid.

Drawing of the Fort Augusta Commandant's House (from an old postcard). Home to the last commandant of the fort, Samuel Hunter, and his family at the end of the war.

the Past" in his *Pennsylvania Fireside Tales Volume 6* for interesting anecdotes about this great chief.) The Great Shamokin Path passed through here and was an important Indian path connecting peoples living along the northern Susquehanna with their counterparts living in the Allegheny River Valley to the west.

The fort was so massive and so formidable in its architectural design that, coupled with its strategic location, it was never subjected to any significant sieges. After the war it gradually disintegrated, but Colonel Hunter, its last commandant, was allowed to stay in the Commandant's Headquarters until his death. His descendants continued to live there until 1848 when the log house burned.

In 1930 the Commonwealth of Pennsylvania purchased the historic property, which is now the headquarters of the Northumberland County Historical Society and its museum. It was through their efforts in 1939 that a small-scale model of the fort was built, then rebuilt in 1974. It reveals just how formidable the fort's defensive ramparts were, and it can be seen today in front of the museum building.[15]

---

15. Information taken from the Northumberland County Historical Society website, https://www.northumberlandcountyhistoricalsociety.org/area-history/fort-Augusta-hunter-house, and from Paul A. W. Wallace, *Indian Paths of Pennsylvania*, 66.

FORT HENDRICKS

Fort Hendricks, also referred to as Schoch's Blockhouse, was built around 1770 by the Hendricks, serving as a place of refuge for settlers in times of trouble with the Indians. Constructed near a spring on Mathias Schoch's land, it was eventually named after him. Despite efforts to preserve it, sometime before 1949 it either fell down, blew over, or was torn down.

A replica of the fort was constructed in 1976, clearly visible from Route 522. In 2014, that replica was moved to its new location, at the Middle Creek Recreation Grounds. The replica can still be seen there today.

There is one interesting episode from the fort's colonial days that deserves repeating here. A description of the blockhouse was included, in the same newspaper article that described this compelling account, that has been handed down as oral history through generations of the Schoch family. As such it is a family heirloom of sorts and is still treasured by the Schoch descendants to this day.

"The Schoch Block House was built in 1770 with logs and having no doors or windows on the first floor, other than the opening thru which the spring water flowed. The first floor contained the fireplace, and remarkable for that day, a plank floor. The second story had a floor of eight-inch logs, hewn square, fitted tightly together with a trap door to the first floor. To the outside was a door made of thick hewed planks, from which a ladder was used to reach the ground. This was drawn up when the inhabitants were within. Only two small openings were at the gable ends. They were eight by twelve inches in size. Whether the family resided in the block house all the time, or in the first cabin, is not known. They, with their neighbors, may have used it only as a refuge."[16]

"Early in the spring of 1776 there stealthily appeared at the block house an old Indian, whom Margaretta, the wife of Mathias, recognized as a friend of her husband. Mathias was away on picket duty. The Indian sat by the fireside throughout the day and would only grunt when spoken to. Late in the afternoon he went away. That evening when Mathias came home his wife told him of the strange visit and how strangely he acted. They decided it bode no good, and Mathias said 'If he comes again try to make him talk.' The next day he came again, and once again the husband was away on picket duty. Margaretta must have had a French woman's

---

16. Agnes Selin Schoch, "Back to Yesteryears," article on Schoch's Blockhouse, *Selinsgrove Times*, October 2, 1939.

Reconstruction of Fort Hendricks, also referred to as Schoch's Blockhouse. The fort was built around 1770. The recontructed version can be seen today at the Middlecreek Township Recreation Grounds at Kreamer, Snyder County Pa.

intuition, for she gave the Indian a bowl of venison soup. He ate it in silence, arose and went to the trap door. He stood there for a long time and then came back to Mrs. Schoch and said she should flee, that the Indians were planning an attack all along the frontier. He also told her not to tell of his visit or the news he brought or he would pay for it with his life.

"The hours seemed endless until Mathias returned home. When Margaretta told him what the Indian said, Mathias took his horse and rode thru the valley telling the news. He and the men prepared for the attack. First all the women and children must be sent south, thru the gap at White Top to their old homes in the lower counties. By daylight, the little train of women and children were on their way south. The men then decided to till the soil by day, attend to their usual picket duty and all gather in the blockhouse by night. That is, all but one family. Across the creek lived the Stock family. They had heard of Indian raids so often that they decided to stay on their farm. That was a great tragedy.

"Peace came at last. The colonies won their battle for Independence and the Indians were subdued and retreated to the western country, and by 1783

REMAINS OF HENDRICK'S BLOCK HOUSE, SNYDER COUNTY.

Lithographic picture of Fort Hendricks as it looked in 1896.

the people returned to Middle Creek valley and once again took up their abodes. History has not revealed the name of the kindly Indian. Margaretta kept her secret well, and she and all the children, other than the Stock family, reached safety and eventually returned to the valley to found families whose descendants today make up the old families of Snyder County."[17]

RICE'S FORT

This frontier outpost, a fortified home built by Abraham and Daniel Rice, could once be seen in Donegal Township near Dutch Fork Lake, Washington County, Pennsylvania. Overlooking Buffalo Creek and not far from the Pennsylvania/West Virginia border, it consisted of three interconnected blockhouses without a stockade fence. It was also well placed defensively, which proved to be a decisive advantage when it was attacked on September 14 and 15, 1782.

Those in the fort had been given advance warning that a band of 100 Indians was seen moving through the area. The warriors were out for blood, having just been defeated in an assault on Fort Henry near Wheeling, West

---

17. Ibid.

Pennsylvania Historical and Museum Commission marker at site of Rice's Fort.

Virginia. Unfortunately for the six men and their families left in the fort, all the other defenders had "gone to Hagerstown to exchange their peltries, for salt, iron, and ammunition."[18]

Expecting an imminent attack, the defenders barely had time to prepare themselves for an onslaught. When the attack came the six men opened fire and drove the attackers back. The assailants surrounded the fort, and throughout the day they attacked again and again. The two sides not only exchanged gunfire during those attacks but reputedly exchanged verbal barbs as well.

The frustrated attackers called to the garrison, "Give up, give up. Indian too many. Indian too big. Give up. Indian no kill."[19]

Unfazed by the taunts, the settlers replied just as boldly, hurling the insult that the Indians were "cowards skulking behind logs; to shew but their yellow hides, and they would make holes in them."[20]

---

18. George Dallas Albert, "The Frontier Forts of Western Pennsylvania," *Report of the Commission to Locate the Site of the Frontier Forts of Pennsylvania, Vol. 2*, Thomas L. Montgomery, editor, 404–10. Also: Alexander Scott Withers, *Chronicles of Border Warfare*, 261–63. Also: Joseph Doddridge, *Notes on the Settlement and Indian Wars of the Western Parts of Virginia and Pennsylvania*, Chapter XXXIV, "Attack on Rice's Fort" 217–21.
19. Ibid.
20. Ibid.

Rice's Fort, was a frontier outpost during the colonial wars. A fortified home consisting of three interconnected blockhouses without a stockade fence, it was built by Abraham and Daniel Rice in Donegal Township near Dutch Fork Lake, Washington County, Pennsylvania. Overlooking Buffalo Creek and not far from the Pennsylvania/West Virginia border, it was also well placed defensively. This photo is of a reconstructed copy of the fort that was made for a 2017 reenactment. It no longer stands today.

Frustrated by the stalwart defenders, the Native Americans at 2 A.M. on September 15, abandoned their attack, leaving four of their dead comrades on the battlefield. However, they exacted their revenge by killing as much livestock as they could find and by destroying and burning surrounding property. Afterwards they broke up into smaller parties and rapidly retreated, thus avoiding capture.

Local resident Conrad Philabaum and a young child were two of the colonial casualties. Conrad's wife Sarah Philabaum recorded a poignant description in her estate papers: "We were all forted at Mr. Rice's and between our cabin and his blockhouse my husband and son fell in the enemy's hand. My husband was scalped, lying in his blood . . . to me a great surprise and affecting sign, the loss of a good husband and an obedient son."[21]

---

21. Information found on "Rice's Fort Historical Marker," https://theclio.com/entry/115244.

Today, a Pennsylvania state historic marker acknowledges the 1782 fight for Rice's Fort. The old bastion no longer exists but a reproduction, which also no longer exists, was created at this spot for a reenactment in 2017.

* * *

Although the reproductions just discussed are nostalgic links to the times of peril and bloodshed our Pennsylvania ancestors had to endure, they are not the real thing. They give us a sense of the colonial period when they were built and why. However, the next chapter introduces three survivors of those times that are remarkable because they are still standing. Included in the chapter are accounts of how effective they were as places of refuge during the times of Pennsylvania's Indian wars.

CHAPTER 7

SURVIVORS OF PENNSYLVANIA'S FRONTIER DAYS

Even though the aforementioned reconstructions are fascinating and have nostalgic links to Pennsylvania's colonial past, it would be even more fascinating and incredible if any of those original bastions still existed and could be personally experienced.

Several buildings are touted as surviving colonial forts, but those claims prove to be suspect, particularly since they are not mentioned in that thorough and well-researched work *The Frontier Forts of Pennsylvania*.

The authors of that exhaustive study, commissioned by Governor Robert E. Pattison in 1893, noted in their final report to Pattison that it "will compare favorably with any heretofore published by the State." On the other hand, they admitted that "There may be errors of opinion, and perchance, errors in fact, but this is to be expected when so little that is reliable has ever been published in regard to the Frontier Forts."[1]

If the authors of that 1895 report had such a scarcity of information upon which they could rely for identifying Pennsylvania's frontier forts, then maybe there are some that they missed. Therefore, those that are described as such today and which are not mentioned in the 1895 report should perhaps not be so easily disregarded. See the End Note for mention of one of them in particular.

---

1. Thomas L. Montgomery, editor, *Report of the Commission to Locate the Site of the Frontier Forts of Pennsylvania, Volume 1, Prefatory Note*, v.

On the other hand, there are forts mentioned in the 1895 report that have survived and which other historical records confirm were indeed bastions used by colonials to protect themselves from Native American war parties. They can still be seen at their original locations. Following are historical details on three of them, some human interest anecdotes that add to their mystique, and photos of what they look like today.

FORT ZELLER

Mentioned in the Frontier Forts of Pennsylvania, Fort Zeller was "built for protection and to guard against attack, the original windows being mere portholes," and it was where "the community found refuge during the Indian troubles, at which time it was said to have been attacked."[2]

It is still standing today, and, according to the Fort Zeller website, "Zeller's Fort or the Heinrich Zeller House is one of the few and rare remaining examples of Germanic Architecture in the Western Hemisphere and is also Pennsylvania's oldest existing fort.[3]

Pioneers who came to the Tulpehocken from the Schoharie valley built it in 1723 and rebuilt it in 1745. Heinrich Zeller's family, their neighbors,

Pennsylvania Historical and Museum Commission marker at Fort Zeller.

---

2. Ibid, 63.
3. www.FortZeller.com

Fort Zeller's spillway where water from a copious spring flows through the canal opening in the basement wall and into the basement.

and the Pennsylvania militia used the fort during the French and Indian War (1754-1763) as refuge and defense against Native American Indian raids. It was actually a fortified house which replaced an earlier log house that was originally built in 1723 near the same location. During the French and Indian War, Lebanon County was susceptible to Native American Indian attacks and many fortifications, forts, and blockhouses were constructed in this area during that time.[4]

A State Historical Marker at the site confirms this information. In addition, there is an interesting legend that is associated with this fort, but, as a word of caution, its origins and factual basis are suspect. However, like most legends, there may be actual historical events upon which it is based,

---

4. www.lebtown.com/2021/08/30/the-heinrich-zeller-house-fort-Zeller-lebanon-countys-secluded-historical-treasure.

Fort Zeller as it looks today in Lebanon County. According to its website, it was here that the community found refuge during the Indian troubles of colonial times, and it is preserved as Pennsylvania's oldest existing colonial fort.

and so I include it herein, leaving it to the reader to decide its authenticity for themselves.

According to the family chronicles, Heinrich Zeller's wife, Christine, was known as "the young countess." It seems to be a title that is in accordance with the Zeller family's royal ascendency, as family genealogy reveals that Heinrich Zeller's mother was Lady Clothilde de Valois Zeller, wife of Jacques Zeller (Salliere) of Deux Ponts, France.[5]

The legend that has been handed down through the Zeller family for generations recounts how one day the "young countess" was home alone. Busily preparing the evening meal, she glanced out one of the foot-wide windows that was one of the few openings in the fort's sturdy foot-thick stone walls. Much to her dismay she saw "three prowling savages"[6] sneaking up the creek (nearby Mill Creek) toward the fort.

Fearing the worst, she immediately hid herself in the cellar near the canal opening where the fort's drinking water flowed naturally from a

---

5. From an inscription on the silver Fort Zeller memorial plaque mounted on a large boulder at the entrance road leading up to Fort Zeller.
6. Thomas L. Montgomery, editor, *Frontier Forts of Pennsylvania*, 63.

copious bedrock spring and into the basement. Guessing that the invaders would attempt to enter the bastion at this, the easiest access point, she prepared herself accordingly. Picking up a large broadax leaning against one of the basement walls, she waited for the first invader.

She did not have to wait long, and when the first brave's head appeared, she brained him with the ax and dragged his body into the basement. She then, by disguising her voice and speaking in the Indians' language "beckoned his companions to follow, which they did; and they were all dispatched in like manner."[7]

Some accounts say that she may have killed as few as three of the invaders, while others indicate maybe as many as six or seven. The exact number is not known, but when Heinrich came back home, his "young countess" helped him bury the dead Indians in the nearby creek bed.

Although this account would seem to be an exaggerated one, given the sagacity and prowess of Native American warriors of that period, it is not without precedent and may be based on an actual event. Over in Greene County in 1779, for example, a similar event is recorded in the history of that county. Here a courageous mother, wielding an ax, supposedly killed three warriors attempting to invade her log cabin home (see the author's chapter titled "Hell hath no Fury", in his *Pennsylvania Fireside Tales Volume 8* for that story).

FORT GADDIS

Considered to be the oldest known log building in Fayette County and the second oldest building in western Pennsylvania (the Fort Pitt blockhouse claiming that distinction), it was most likely constructed by Thomas Gaddis in 1769–74 to be his cabin home. He oversaw the defense of the region, and his home was both a site for community meetings and a shelter in times of emergency.

As such it was often referred to as Fort Gaddis. Located along the Catawba Trail, an important north-south New York to Tennessee Indian path, it offered Fayette County settlers some protection in case any of those aboriginal travelers decided to attack.

It was added to the National Register of Historic Places in 1974 as the Thomas Gaddis Homestead. Gaddis later served as a colonel in the

---

7. Ibid.

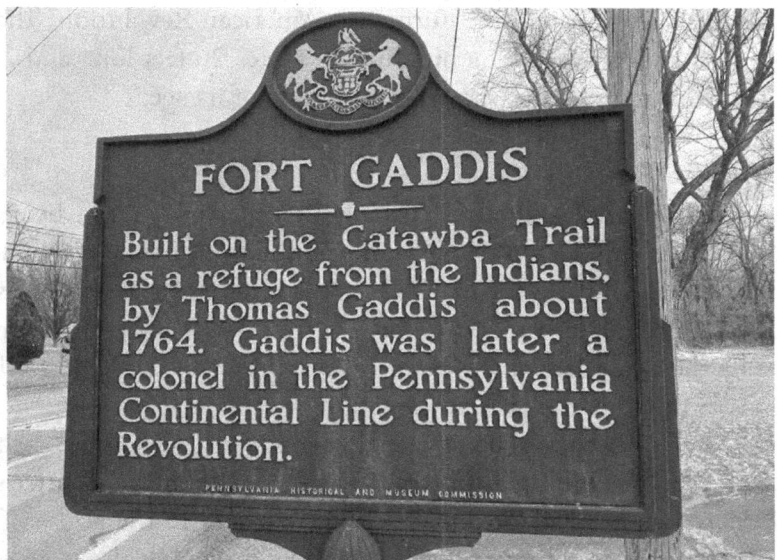

Pennsylvania Historical and Museum Commission marker at Fort Gaddis.

Fort Gaddis as it looks today. It survives as as one of the last standing colonial frontier log forts in Pennsylvania. Picture taken by the author in 2025.

Pennsylvania Continental Line during the American Revolution. The one-and-a half-story, one-room log building measures 26 feet long and 20 feet wide. It is still standing but showing the effects of its age.[8]

LIGHT'S FORT

Still withstanding the buffeting currents of time, it can still be seen in the town of Lebanon, Lebanon County. Built by Johannes Peter Leicht (later known as John Light) in 1742, it is sometimes referred to as Fort Leicht, but also in later years as Light's Fort. In 1896 it was mentioned as follows by the compilers of the *Frontier Forts of Pennsylvania*. Referring to the times of the Indian troubles, they state:

"The town of Lebanon, being already densely settled, was resorted to as a place of safety for hundreds of families who fled from the frontier settlements. Sixty families had, at one time, taken shelter in the house of John Light, which is still standing, and known among the people there as the 'Old Fort' . . . It was a house of refuge, having still the arched vault under the first floor, spacious enough to shelter comfortably one hundred people."[9]

Just like Fort Zeller, Light's Fort also has a legend associated with it that comes down from those terrible times of warfare between colonials and Native Americans. Similar to the Fort Zeller account, however, those demanding solid evidence may have a basis for questioning this account's

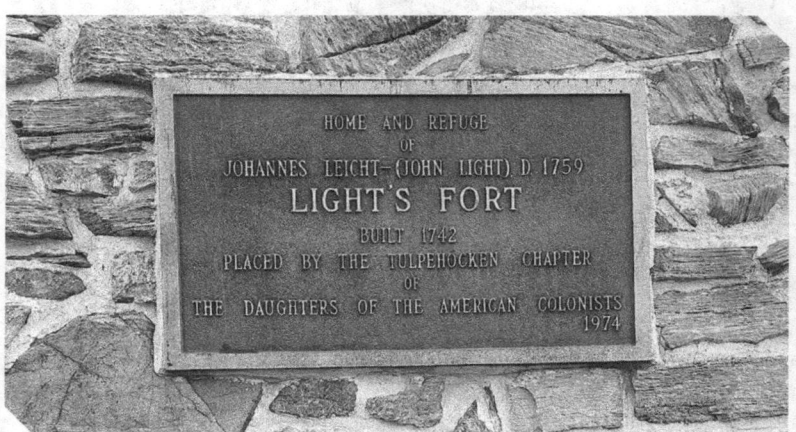

Historical plaque on a wall of Fort Leicht giving some details about its history and preservation (photo courtesy of Lawrence Knorr).

---

8. Found on the "National Historic Landmarks Register of Historic Places in Pennsylvania," and at https://www.loc.gov/item/pa1916/.

9. Thomas L. Montgomery, editor, *Frontier Forts of Pennsylvania*, 62.

Fort Leicht, also called Light's Fort since it was also the home of John Light, served as a place of safety for hundreds of families who fled from the frontier settlements during Indian incursions into Lebanon County. It still stands today in the city of Lebanon, where it is sometimes referred to as the 'Old Fort' (photo courtesy of Lawrence Knorr).

authenticity as well. The tale seems to be uncomfortably brutal for our present-day sensibilities, but like the Zeller tale, there may be some supporting historical precedents that lend it some measure of credence.

It is not mentioned in any of the standard histories of that era. No mention of the fort can be found in Sipe's *Indian Wars*, Withers' *Chronicles*, or Loudon's *Narratives*, or in Lebanon, Berks, Lancaster, or other nearby county histories. It is therefore most likely an oral account preserved in the Light family chronicles.

The tale starts in 1757 with John Light's daughter, Marcella. One day the kind-hearted lady saw a young native woman outside the fort who appeared to be hungry and shivering in the cold winter air. Taking pity upon her, Marcella brought her inside to the warmth of the fort and, after feeding her, told her she could spend the night in an upstairs room.

In the middle of that night, Marcella was awakened by the sound of the native girl sneaking downstairs. She followed her out into the cold and dark night, and into their barn. Here she observed her setting a number of small fires to burn the barn down. She immediately attacked the girl, knocked her out and put out the fires.

She then rushed inside and told her father what had happened. The old settler, angered by this deception and by the lack of appreciation for their hospitality, handed Marcella a knife and told her to go back to the barn and kill the malicious visitor.

Several days later the Lights discovered evidence of a recent Indian encampment. The blackened embers of the Indian campfires and the fresh footprints visible in the mud indicated that they had been there just days ago, no doubt hoping to ambush the family as they were fighting to save their burning barn. However, thanks to Marcella's keen eyes and her vengeful actions, the Lights were spared both those tragedies.[10]

It's hard for us to believe that a young lady of any era could be so proficient with a knife; skilled enough to kill something with it. However, as mentioned before, these were difficult times that often required desperate measures to survive, and there is at least one historical account showing that colonial maids may have been up to the task when necessity required it.

See the author's chapter titled "Wolf Days in Centre County" in his *Pennsylvania Fireside Tales Volume 8* for a tale about how one settler's brave daughter saved him from a losing struggle he was having with a big gray wolf by killing it with a large knife she retrieved from their Lancaster County log cabin.

These kinds of human-interest stories must also have been told about some of the other Pennsylvania colonial forts whose sites are marked by blue and gold Pennsylvania State Historical Commission markers. Those wishing to find them can get a booklet from that commission which identifies all those markers and their locations. Their tales might also be found in the histories of the area where they once stood.

SPANGLER'S BLOCKHOUSE

This sandstone relic was a remarkable landmark connecting the present day with Pennsylvania's Colonial past. It is no longer a survivor of those days, however, but is worthy of mention in this chapter anyway, because it stood the test of time well into the twentieth century. Also, because your author saw it many times and got a photo of it.

---

10. Ibid.

Built in 1764, the Fort Pitt Block House is all that remains of Fort Pitt, one of the largest and most elaborate British forts in North America and a key defense during the French and Indian War.

Unfortunately, however, in 1967 an Amish farmer purchased the farm property, and decided to knock the fort down, using its stones as landfill around the foundation of his new house. And this, despite entreaties from the excavator and bulldozer contractors he had hired to do the job and from many locals. All pleaded with him to let the fortress stand, but their pleas fell on deaf ears. Fortunately, however, a photo of the structure has survived, and descriptions of it have also been preserved in various publications.

For instance, in an excerpt from a 1930s *Centre Daily Times of State College* newspaper article (date not certain), Reverend J. J. Weaver wrote the following:

> "There still remains the Block House on the farm now owned by Mr. O. F. Stover, 2 miles east of Rebersburg. It is still in a fine state of preservation . . . The old fort was erected before the year 1800 on land owned by Christopher Spangler, who acquired this land with others from various individuals. . . .

"Now as to the old Block House or fort, for such it was, erected by presumably Christopher Spangler, for protection against marauding bands of Indians, who at that time were mostly in the western part of Pennsylvania but who made incursions to the central and eastern portions of the state to steal if they so willed to murder some unsuspecting whites . . .

"It is built of mountain sandstone with the following dimensions: 10 ft. wide x 13 ft. long, 10 ft. high, walls 2 ft. 4" thick. There are two floors, both with very low ceilings. On the upper floor there are 7 loop holes through which rifles could be used against an enemy. 2 loop holes on each of the east, west, and southern walls, and one that faces the north. On the outer edge these loop holes or slits in the wall are filled in by placing small stones therein, so the old building could be used as a smoke house to smoke meat.

"There are two heavy doors on the western side, for this faced the original house, which stood just a few feet south of the present large stone house erected in 1805. A building of the proportions of this Block House would scarcely give protection, but to one family, for which it was unquestionably erected. This writer has visited many old fort sites and some buildings that were used as forts in Indian days, but none are so well preserved as the little Spangler Block House."

Unfortunately, the fort could have been saved in 1956 before it was destroyed in 1967 had the Centre County Historical Society been more far-sighted. In one of their publications, they described the situation as follows:

"The Centre County Historical Society has been offered the gift of a little building which, probably more than any other in the County, is a monument to the very real dangers early settlers of this area faced from hostile Indians. The structure is a 10 by 13 foot blockhouse made of mountain sandstone on a farm now owned by Ralph Confer, about two miles east of Rebersburg . . .

Spangler's Fort was erected by Christopher Spangler, for protection against marauding bands of Indians. This sandstone relic in Centre County was a remarkable landmark connecting the present day with Pennsylvania's Colonial past. It unfortunately was destroyed by an Amish farmer when he bought the property.

"Mr. Confer has offered to deed to County Historical Society the building, a ten-foot plot of ground around it and access way across his property to the site. He seems anxious to clear the way for the preservation of the structure as an historical landmark . . . the building is the only one known to exist in Centre County built specifically for protection against Indians."

The Centre County Historical Society did not accept the offer to save the Spangler Fort. It was too far off the highway (today Route 192), and the County didn't want to maintain the road (1/2 mile lane) for people to visit the site."[11]

---

11. Paul Dubbs, "The Blockhouse Near Rebersburg," *Centre County Heritage* (publication of the Centre County Historical Society), *Volume 1, Number 2*, May 1956.

It is almost criminal how the preservation of this important piece of history slipped through so many fingers and was lost to us forever. With its loss went a chance to experience what it would have been like to stand shoulder to shoulder with the brave frontiersmen who might have sheltered here during an Indian attack.

NOTE: There is one fort in particular that is not mentioned in *Frontier Forts of Pennsylvania*, but which locals believe should have been included.

Located at 4333 Linglestown Road along the Blue Mountain in Dauphin County, the building now serves as a family home and so no longer resembles a fortress in any way; aluminum siding and various additions have altered its appearance over the years. A nearby sign along the roadside describes it as follows:

FORT GILCRIST

Fort Gilchrist, still in its original location and partially restored in 1946, is located on Linglestown Road. The structure was originally built as a one-and-a-half-story log fort, featuring 24 "Heavenly Lord Hinges," hinges in the shape of the letters "HL". It was believed that these hinges kept the witches out.

Inspections by local historians have not found evidence that this was once a fort, but locals are convinced it was, particularly since it may have once been a headquarters for the Paxton Rangers. On the other hand, history records that those Scotch-Irish Presbyterian frontiersmen were organized by Reverend John Elder and were stationed at Fort Patton near Linglestown. Nonetheless, officials in Paxton Township of Dauphin County noted in their latest Comprehensive Plan brochure:

As colonists began to disperse west from the Delaware River Valley to pursue agriculture in the valleys, they encountered Native Americans on many occasions. A semi-organized group of men, known as the Paxton Rangers, defended new settlements from Indians as the frontier advanced westward. After numerous confrontations with the Native Americans, the colonists purchased the land south of Blue Mountain, between the Delaware and Susquehanna Rivers in 1732, though disputes continued.

As a result, a string of forts was constructed to defend the settlers and to block travel routes across Blue Mountain. This line of defense included

Fort Patton and Fort Barnett in Lower Paxton Township, as well as Fort Gilchrist and Fort Berryhill beyond the Township boundaries. The forts were later used throughout the French and Indian Wars.[12]

The Pennsylvania State Historical and Museum Commission has not placed one of their historical markers here because they consider it to be of local interest only, instead of having statewide historical interest. They base that claim on the fact that it was only a fortified private home with no colonial troops ever being stationed there. It was used only as a place of refuge by locals during times of Indian incursions.[13]

LOCATIONS, ETC.: locations and GPS coordinates of all the forts mentioned in this chapter can be found via Internet searches.

---

12. Paxton Township Supervisors, "Lower Paxton Comprehensive Plan, Chapter 1: Introduction to Lower Paxton Township."
13. William Minsker, email dated February 2, 2025.

CHAPTER 8

LANDMARK PLACE NAMES

In compiling this volume, I continued to find Pennsylvania placenames that cried out for explanation. Many such names were addressed in previous volumes (see the Chapter titled "What's In a Name" in the author's *Pennsylvania Fireside Tales Volume 6*, and the chapter titled "Pig's Ear? Yellow Dog? Torpedo? Gum Stump?" in *Pennsylvania Fireside Tales Volume 8*), and these new ones were just as compelling and unique as those previous ones. Like those others, they also called out to me to find out the story behind them; so, since they are landmarks of a sort, what better place to do so than as a separate chapter in *Pennsylvania Mountain Landmarks Volume 5*.

BROAD AXE

Named after the Broad Axe Inn, an old stone tavern which is still standing in Ambler, along the Butler Pike near Blue Bell Pennsylvania in Montgomery County. The Inn has a remarkable history and, until closing in 2019, was considered one of the oldest, if not the oldest, taverns in the entire country. The Inn was named after its tavern sign, which featured a compass, a square, and one of the large wide axes lumbermen used to cut down trees during their lumbering operations. It has a rather uncertain history, shrouded in myth and legend.

The exact year it was built and by whom is unknown. Some say it was erected in 1681,[1] the year William Penn arrived in the state that would

---
1. www.oldestbarineverystate.com/the-bars/Pennsylvania-the-broad-axe-tavern

eventually be named after him. Others say it was built in 1792. The latter date being the least probable since the Inn was mentioned in a newspaper article published in the *Pennsylvania Gazette*, on June 20, 1771, where it was stated that it was here that "two stray horses were being kept until their owners could be found." Then also, there are many legendary accounts associating the inn with events that occurred during the Revolutionary War.

Legends and stories about the place even predate the Revolutionary War, since it was built alongside on old Indian path which eventually would become today's Butler Pike. It was on this road that farmers would haul their grain to be ground at local mills, and on which, according to the Inn's history Derrick Van Pelt, the Inn's owner in 1763, began to run horse races.

Van Pelt's business grew as a result, with bettors celebrating or bemoaning their wins or losses at the tavern bar. Old records of the Inn's bar tabs show that many of those patrons were men who later served in the Revolutionary War. It is their stories that connect the Inn with the latter years of the 1770s, the years of the Revolutionary War, that hold the greatest fascination for historians.

Unlike many taverns of that period, the Broad Axe managed to remain open. Many inns closed due to lack of food and the large numbers of hungry British and colonial soldiers stopping to beg for something to eat. The Broad Axe, on the other hand, had at that time become such a community focal point that it was regularly patronized by locals. They considered it not only as a place to get a hearty meal, but as a gathering place to exchange gossip and to hear the news read from local newspapers. Travelers also knew it was a warm and comfortable place to stay for the night. Local lore suggests, and is confirmed by entries in local diaries and in letters describing it, that among those passersby was General George Washington, who is believed to have marched past the Inn with his troops at least half a dozen times.

Local lore also maintains that one of the patrons at the tavern at this time was British General James Grant. After imbibing too freely of the tavern's spirits, the general while "in his cups" inadvertently spoke of the British plan to kidnap French general Marquis de Lafayette, hero and molder of the colonial army, in order to embarrass the French. Shortly after being informed of the plot, Lafayette managed to escape, only to survive and subsequently lead American forces to victory.

There is also an interesting account describing the first time Washington and his troops marched by the tavern. It occurred immediately following the Battle of Germantown, on October 4, 1777, which proved to be a rout of the colonials. British and Hessian soldiers chased the retreating American soldiers down Skippack Road, as Butler Pike was then known, past the Broad Axe and to where the American Cavalry under General Pulaski was waiting for them, at present-day Blue Bell Inn. There a fierce firefight ensued with many injured and dead soldiers falling on the field of battle. Charging and retreating soldiers ran back and forth, many dying along the roadside, including a section in front of the Broad Axe. After that fight, both armies declared a cease fire and buried their dead alongside the road in unmarked graves where they lie at rest today.

After the war there were many reports of people encountering the restless spirits of those dead and buried soldiers. Moreover, there were many other Revolutionary soldiers buried along other roads leading to the tavern and in the woods surrounding it. Those facts, coupled with the area being often shrouded in thick white mists, tweaked the imaginations of those inclined to believe in otherworldly spirits, and do so yet today.[2]

BUCKHORN

Native Americans developed their own system of "highways" through the dense forests of Pennsylvania. Their pathways often followed animal trails, since the animals using the paths instinctively sought out the easiest routes to navigate. There were many Indian paths crisscrossing Pennsylvania, some more heavily used than others, but all were well blazed with various markers leading from one village to another. Those same pathways eventually became bridle paths, then wagon paths, and finally roadways for practical colonists who appreciated the navigational advantages offered by the routes.

One major trail known as the Great Warriors' Path extended from Sunbury, Northumberland County, passed through Bloomsburg in Columbia County, and then headed northward to Tioga, Tioga County. It was a major warpath in times of war, but also heavily used in times of peace

---

2. Unknown author, "Broadaxe Tavern," *Nightlife Magazine*, July 21, 2018.

since it was "fed by Indian highways from all parts of the Six Nations home country."[3] It was perhaps one of these "feeders" of the Great Warrior Path northwest of Bloomsburg that had a trail marker that was widely known as the "buckhorn tree."[4]

The old oak tree stood at the edge of a swamp near the small settlement that grew up here. Hanging in one of the branches of the oak was a set of buck antlers that the Indians had placed there to mark this spot. It was an important juncture where a path from the forts and settlements in the south merged with a path to the North Mountain region. Located just northwest of Bloomsburg, the trailway later became a road that led through a small community that grew up here. Eventually that small hamlet came to be called Buckhorn, after the unusual Indian trail marker.

As time passed, however, the tree grew around the antlers, eventually covering them over entirely. Decades flew by and the trail marker which gave the town its name became a distant memory, acquiring legendary qualities, as though it had never existed. Thus it stood for many decades until the tree's secret was finally revealed.

One account says that "a lightning bolt split the tree open in front of the hotel around 1900, and the weathered buck horn was exposed!"[5] Yet another claims that in the early 1870s "a woodpecker reopened the wound in the tree and revealed the truth of what was then considered simply a tradition." The interesting relic was retrieved and is said to have been placed in a museum at Allentown.[6] It may reside there yet today and will be added to this writer's list of things to track down. A picture of this old landmark would be a nice addition to his collection.

CHERRY TREE

This small village in Indiana County now goes by the name of Cherry Tree, but when first settled in 1822, the pioneers called it Canoe Place, from the name the Iroquois had bestowed upon it. To those native sons, this was just another "Ganneuc" or "place of the canoe."[7] The Indians used canoes to navigate the Susquehanna River, but at some points it was so shallow that

---

3. Paul A. W. Wallace, *Indian Paths of Pennsylvania*, 72.
4. J. H. Beers, *Historical and Biographical Annals of Columbia and Montour Counties, Pennsylvania*, 239–40.
5. From *A History of the Early Brobst/Probst Families in Pennsylvania*, found at https://homepages.rootsweb.com/~brobst/chronicles/chap3.htm
6. J. H. Beers, *Historical and Biographical Annals of Columbia and Montour Counties, Pennsylvania*, 239–40.
7. J. T. Stewart, *History of Indiana County Pennsylvania*, Volume 1, 550.

they had to leave the river and carry their canoes (portage them) on land, until they could reenter the river where it became navigable again.

Canoe Place was the village title that prevailed until residents agreed to change its name in 1907. By that time the lumbermen had cleared away much of the vast forests that had originally cloaked the valleys and mountain tops of the Allegheny Plateau. Canoe Place had been a center of that thriving lumber industry in the late nineteenth century. Surprisingly, however, there was one huge tree still standing at the mouth of Cush Cushion Creek where it drained into the West Branch of the Susquehanna. The huge cherry tree, which was a survivor of the original virgin forest, had somehow escaped the lumberman's axe, perhaps because of its historical significance.

Its historical significance wasn't lost to locals, who wanted to pay homage to it. So, when they decided to change their town's name in 1907, Cherry Tree was the name they chose. The tree had served as an important landmark, marking the northern corner of the land purchase between the Penn family and the Iroquois following the Treaty of Fort Stanwix in 1768. It had also been where Colonel John Armstrong and his military expedition of 300 men had encamped on their way to destroy the Indian town of Kittanning in 1779.

The spot where it grew at Canoe Place is now marked by a gold and blue Pennsylvania Historical and Museum Commission historical signpost. A community monument, dedicated in 1894, can also be seen near the site of the original cherry tree. It no longer proudly lifts its flowered limbs to the sky in the springtime. By 1830 the ground around it had been eroded away by frequent spring floods, and, absent sustaining nourishment, the old tree finally was washed away by those same floods.[8]

So, Cherry Tree has nothing to do with George Washington and his cherry tree. Nonetheless, there was another man who lived here who was, during the nineteenth century lumbering era, almost as famous as our first president. This was because of his outrageous personality and even more so because of his outrageous exploits. His fame spread far and wide during his lifetime. You might say that he is still a landmark of sorts, not of the physical variety, but a cultural one.

Born in Muncy, Lycoming County, in 1805, his family moved to Cherry Tree when he was thirteen. Here he became fascinated with the lifestyles of

---

8. See: Visitindianacountypa.org/members/a-brief-history-of-indiana-county/

the "woods hicks" who wielded the axes and crosscut saws to fell the forest giants that grew in the trackless forests surrounding his hometown.

He was a natural born lumberjack, and his large stature allowed him to join that elite fraternity. Standing at six-foot-three and weighing 200 pounds with a bushy face beard that made him even more intimidating, Joseph McCreery was hailed as someone who was as strong as an ox and somewhat of a superman, who could easily perform seemingly impossible tasks. His superhuman feats soon became a popular topic in the folk tales that were told around Cherry Tree, and they were soon elevated to the "tall" variety.[9]

Cherry Tree Joe, as Joseph McCreery became known, was soon a folk hero, not only in Indiana County, but from coast to coast as his tales spread to other lumbering camps throughout the United States. There are some today who even think that it was Cherry Tree Joe who inspired tellers of tall tales in the lumber camps to invent a mythical hero who became the famous Paul Bunyan.

Bunyan, like Cherry Tree Joe, was a giant of a man whose exaggerated exploits seem to resemble those once attributed to Cherry Tree Joe. It is believed that Joe was a member of the crew that manned the first lumber raft to be floated down the Susquehanna in 1827. While this part of his life is undoubtedly true, many other of the exploits attributed to him seem to be of the Bunyanesque variety. For example, there is one about the time Cherry Tree Joe single-handedly broke up a ten-mile log jam, and then after breaking up yet another, whittled the logs into little sticks. Paul Bunyan's catalog of feats includes this same tale, and both his and Cherry Tree Joe's conclude "and that's how toothpicks were invented!"[10]

It was said his eyesight was so sharp that he could "take a raft downriver in the dark." There were other similar feats attributed to Cherry Tree Joe, like the time a large timber raft was hung up on a rocky shelf in the river. Undaunted by its size, Joe managed to lift it up single-handedly and then set it back down in navigable water. He then nonchalantly jumped aboard as though he was ready for some leisure time following such an extraordinary show of strength.[11]

---

9. Mike Reuther, "Cherry Tree Joe was a man among men," *Williamsport Sun-Gazette*, March 5, 2018.
10. Ibid.
11. Ibid.

Another superhuman feat attributed to Joe was said to have occurred during the Johnstown Flood of 1889. Seeing a large house riding on the raging floodwater, Joe pulled it onto the riverbank, later finding that by doing so he had saved the lives of two sets of triplets trapped inside.[12]

His personal life was also the subject of similar fictitious tales. These folktales say that Joe's wife "cooked on a skillet six feet square, used a side of bacon to grease it, and a barrel of flour every morning to make his flapjacks." It was from this quantity of food supplies, say the same folktales, that "the mice in his cabin grew to weigh 60 pounds and why he then had to keep a panther as a house cat!"[13]

In real life McCreery was no slouch. He was known as a natural athlete, both agile and quick. It was also said of him that he was quite the "ladies' man," but nonetheless he did settle on one woman and took her as a wife. To Eleanor Banks he had eight children—all boys, and from them he had six grandchildren, 24 great-grandchildren, and 23 great-great-grandchildren. In 1861 he heeded the call and, at age 56, enlisted in the 11th Pennsylvania Volunteer Calvary. During one of that unit's engagements, Joe lost a leg and was discharged. Thereafter he became somewhat short-tempered and as a result became known as "contrary Joe."[14]

He died in bed at age 90 in 1895. Contrary to his wishes, he died without his boots on, but at the annual Raftsmen's Association reunions, his hobnailed boots were always displayed to honor the man who had worn them. They held this place of honor until the association was finally dissolved in 1955, with the cry "The cheery hail of 'Land! Tie up!' to be heard no more, forever, upon these rivers."[15] Queries to local Indiana County historical societies and offices to locate the whereabouts of Joe's boots today proved to be fruitless.

FREE LOVE VALLEY

Although this may sound like a place that was popular during the hedonistic era of the "Swinging Sixties," with its sexual liberation and psychedelic adventures, it was not like another Woodstock. Its roots date back much further than that; so far back in fact that most people living here today have

---

12. Clark Creery, *Exploits of Cherry Tree Joe McCreery*, found on WikiTree genealogical site at https://www.wikitree.com/wiki/McCreery-331.
13. Ibid.
14. Homer Tope Rosenberger, *Mountain Folks*, 195.
15. Ibid.

no clue as to the origins of that intriguing place name. The only evidence that such a place existed at all, in Coventry Township of northern Chester County, is that its name appears on a few old and scarce maps of that county.

Likewise, as might be expected, there are few landmarks in this valley that provide any clues as to why it is so named. There really are no such landmarks, but the churches that existed at the time the name arose are still active churches, and as such, still give us a tenuous link to the religious sect from which this curious name arose. The sect's story is mentioned in an early history of Chester County, which described it in lurid details as follows:

"There existed in Chester County in 1840, and perhaps a few years earlier, a most strange sect, bearing the equally strange title of 'Battle Axes'. They had a number of followers in the northern part of the county in 1840, at which time they seem first to have attracted attention. In 1844, a number of them were arrested; some of whom were tried and convicted, the others being subsequently discharged. William Stubblebine seems to have died in this faith, and in the case (Snyder vs. Stubblebine) regarding the validity of his will there is a mention of this sect. Its principles were essentially those known as 'free love', the leading ideas being that all connection between husband and wife were severed, and to possess all things in common, in the fullest sense of the words. The leader of the society was Theophilus R. Gates, then a resident of Philadelphia, and the chief female votary one Hannah Williamson, a single woman. It is unnecessary to add that this peculiar sect has now no existence here."[16]

As might be expected, this counter-cultural sect created quite a scandal among their staid conservative neighbors, many of whom had been fellow congregants in the churches once attended by the Battle Axes. The conservative farm families and local authorities were shocked by the sect's immoral beliefs and actions. That they were nudists was bad enough, but when they bathed nude in local ponds the local authorities arrested them. However, the proverbial "straw that broke the camel's back" was the day in 1843 when they paraded, in their natural state, up and down the aisles of the Shenkel Church while gleefully waving their arms in the air. It may have been at that time that the Temple Methodist church, about a mile down

---

16. J. Smith Futhey and Gilbert Cope, *History of Chester County, Pennsylvania*, 301.

the road, was founded to encourage the group to abandon their immoral beliefs and actions; to "bring them religion." Also to dissuade them from meeting at each other's homes to conduct their "services," which, it was believed, were done in the same *au naturale* state as that of Adam and Eve.[17]

It may also have been at that point that the valley got its name. Historical accounts indicate that this may be the case since one of the sect's core beliefs was that conventional marriage repressed the natural urges of both sexes. That both would be happier coupling with anyone and whenever they desired to do so. Further, they believed that there needed to be no commitments involved between those who made such connections. They also believed that these were not immoral beliefs because this was God's will. To locals the name Free Love Valley may have seemed to be an appropriate title for the valley at this point since it perhaps was a way to exhibit the scorn they felt for their sinful neighbors.[18]

The leader and founder of the "Battle Axes" was Theophilus R. Gates, whose charisma attracted several dozen followers. He called his group "The Battle Axes of the Lord," which led others to refer to his followers as Battle Axes. Gates, born in 1787, was typical of the cult leaders of today, easily converting his flock into staunch adherents of his dogma, while lacing it with sexual overtones. His adherents eventually declined, and as his cult shrunk and the resistance to it grew, Gates' health declined until he died in 1846 aged 59. A small white headstone marks his burial spot in Union Cemetery along Route 74 in Parker Ford. Those who wish to know more about Free Love Valley and the Battle Axes should read the book by Charles Coleman Sellers titled *Theophilus the Battle-Axe*.[19]

FROZEN RUN

A tributary of Hemlock Creek in Columbia County, Pennsylvania. The first serious efforts to manufacture pig iron, from the iron ore deposits discovered at the mouth of this stream at an earlier date, were begun by the New York Coal and Iron Company of Elmira, New York, in 1831. Six years later a charcoal furnace was erected a short distance up Frozen Run to process ore from the nearby Red Run mines. Since that ore was quite impure, it was allowed to freeze over the winter. "This allowed the fire, clay,

---

17. https://jmtomko.wordpress.com/2009/08/06/weird-history-free-love-valley-and-the-battle-axes/.
18. Elizabeth Humphrey, "From Farm Community to Haven for Free Sexual Affairs," *Sunday Local News*, West Chester, Pennsylvania, March 29, 1987.
19. https://jmtomko.wordpress.com/2009/08/06/weird-history-free-love-valley-and-the-battle-axes/.

and ore to be separated manually—thus the name Frozen Run."[20] The smelted product was known as "charcoal iron," and it was valued because of its heat resistance, toughness, and malleability.[21]

GALLOWS RUN

A small stream that rises on the southern slope of Buckwampum Mountain in Springfield Township of Bucks County. Near here was the site of a Delaware Indian village known as Pechoqueolin, one of the largest native villages in the county. However, the name for the stream was not originally connected to this village nor to Native Americans at all; but popularly thought to have come from the fact that the body of a man who committed suicide was found hanging from a tree on the hillside at the mouth of the creek. Subsequently it was accepted that the names for the hillside, Gallows Hill, and its creek, were based on that morbid discovery.

However, that was later debunked by local historians who claimed that the name came from a man's suspenders! Another name for them in colonial days was trouser braces or gallowses, which came from the structure, two upright posts and a crossbeam, or gallows, used to hang criminals. Eventually that term was used to refer to any similar structure used for supporting or suspending something.[22]

The Bucks County pundits stated that it was a pair of those gallowses hanging on a tree branch at the run that led to its name. They were placed there, said the locals, by Edward Marshall, one of the runners of the Penn Family's infamous "Walking Purchase" of 1737 (see the chapter titled "Guardian of the Trail" in the author's *Pennsylvania Fireside Tales Volume 3* for more information on this shameful event), when his suspenders broke as he jumped across the creek. Marshall took them off and hung them on a tree branch at this spot along the creek rather than being burdened by them as he continued his headlong rush. Subsequently, locals found them still hanging there and decided to name the creek from this unusual discovery.[23]

Those who pass on the story of the broken trouser braces do not explain how fast Marshall might have been able to run while holding up his trousers with one hand so that they did not fall down around his ankles!

---

20. Michael Bressler, "The Wild Lycoming—Stream of History," *Journal of the Lycoming County Historical Society, Volume VII Winter-Spring Number One, 1970–1971*, page 23.
21. Michael Williams, *Deforesting The Earth*, 316.
22. George MacReynolds, *Place Names in Bucks County, Pennsylvania*, 183.
23. Ibid.

INTERCOURSE

Anyone who has traveled through the Pennsylvania Dutch Counties of Lancaster, Lebanon, Berks, and York in southeastern Pennsylvania will no doubt recall passing through towns with suggestive names like Virginville, Paradise, Blue Ball, Fertility, Lititz, and Bareville, and others. As a resident of Lancaster County for some years I often explored this region, enjoying its delightful countryside. Picturesque Amish farms and extensive fields of green and gold never failed to make those trips pleasurable. In addition, the unique names of the small villages and towns always proved to be a delight as well. Tourists visiting the region find those names novel and delightful too, but the town of Intercourse is probably remembered most of all. It is a source of fun for locals also, who over the years liked to jokingly tell travelers "If you want to get to Paradise you've got to go through Intercourse!"

That's a bit of an exaggeration since there is more than one way to get to the village of Paradise in Paradise Township without passing through nearby Intercourse in Leacock Township. Nonetheless, the pithy remark was always sure to elicit a chuckle, and no doubt still does today. On the other hand, those same tourists would then often, I'm sure, inquire about the seemingly suggestive name of the town called Intercourse. How did that name arise, and does it have any sexual connotations at all?

This small Amish community sits at the junction of two major highways and several smaller ones, just as it did back in the early nineteenth century, when horse and buggy traffic converged here to shop at what was then the commercial center of the area. The pace of life was much slower back in those days, and so shoppers took the time to engage in friendly conversations and neighborly visits. A common term then for pleasant fellowship and frequent engagement with friends and family was "friendly intercourse." Intercourse was also a term applied to any trading center where such interactions occurred. Hence, one local "wag" thought it was a good name for the town that grew up here. His name, according to historians of the area, was George Brungard.[24]

There have been other theories offered as to basis for the town's odd name, which was originally Cross Keys. One such theory is based on the fact that the town stood at the crossroads of two key roads that intersected here: the Newport Pike (a north-south highway linking Wilmington,

---

24. https://www.discoverlancaster.com/blog/wacky-town-names-lancaster/.

Delaware, and Erie, Pennsylvania—now Route 772) and the old King's Highway, a cross-state thoroughfare linking Philadelphia and Pittsburgh—now Old Philadelphia Pike, Route 340.) However, six- to eight-bell teams of horses were a common sight here in the eighteenth century. Loaded with supplies and freight they regularly made round trips between the two cities. All along the route taverns sprang up to provide rest and refreshment for weary and thirsty horses and travelers.

These rest stops also became social centers where people could exchange news and gossip and transact their business. One of those taverns, a log building built in 1754, was the first building constructed at Intercourse, and it was its tavern sign bearing the image of two crossed keys, that some believe was the basis for the town's original name.[25]

However, the history of the area also recalls that there was a racetrack near here as well. It was a mile-long straightaway starting at the east end of town. At its entrance was a sign marking its entryway with the lettering "Entercourse." It was this name, some believe, that gradually morphed into "Intercourse," and which became the name locals used when referring to the settlement.[26]

The little community continues to thrive today, with its greatest claim to fame being that it was the filming location for the 1985 Amish thriller titled *Witness*, starring Harrison Ford. Its other distinction seems to be that it cannot keep its town name signposts. They are irresistible souvenirs which are regularly stolen by those who want them, it would have to be assumed, for their own disreputable purposes. However, the thieves might be disappointed to learn that when George Brungard named the town back in 1813, it had nothing to do with his sex life!

NOODLE DOOSIE

Sounding like a fictional town from a comic book, there was once an actual place in West Earl Township of Lancaster County that had this name. It created a worldwide sensation when a local newsman published an article about it in a Lancaster newspaper back in 1998. Other news outlets, intrigued by the unusual title, picked up the story, and to the surprise of the newsman, "the world experienced Noodle Doosie-mania."[27]

25. Author unknown, "Intercourse," *Amish Country News* magazine, *Holiday 2024, Winter 2025* issue.
26. Ibid.
27. https://lancasteronline.com/opinion/noodle-doosie-cant-get-there-from-here/article_61257117-76a3-5fc3-8b47-58626624ddad.html.

Despite the furor, very few locals at that time still referred to their town by that name. Founded in the 1700s, townspeople had decided centuries later that the name should be changed, since it would otherwise subject them to ridicule when they had to say it when someone asked them where they were from. It sounded too ridiculous, and others thought it was too hard to pronounce. And so it was that Noodle Doosie became Napierville.

The change of names, however, did not erase the history behind the odd title and the explanation for that strange name in the first place. History was never clear on the subject, but despite the name change, the local Pennsylvania Dutchmen kept that memory alive in their local folklore. One of their most popular explanations being that it arose from a situation involving two zealous men courting, or "noodling" in their vernacular, then fighting over the same woman.

Perhaps their fights were, as they are sometimes described, real "doosies." Nonetheless, the history of the town and its surroundings has preserved details of other incidents that occurred here that, although not of the pugilistic variety, some may agree could also be described as doosies. Perhaps it was the combination of the story of the noodling men and the frequency of incidents of the doosie variety that led to the strange name. In fact, it might be conjectured that it was nothing more than some locals with an "antic" nature, as those with a humorous side were sometimes described in those days, coming up with the title in jest, chuckling to themselves as it came to be more popular when referring to the town.

But as to the other colorful incidents that may have inspired the town's name, there were several notable ones that occurred at a nearby local watering hole known as *Die Rotie Kuh*, or The Red Cow. It was a place where all kinds of shenanigans occurred, at least in the memory of those who once patronized it, and one of the favorite ones involved a former Hessian soldier named General Willembrock, who decided to permanently settle in this area some thirty years after being taken prisoner at either the Battle of Trenton or the Battle of Saratoga while fighting for England in the Revolutionary War.

It's recalled that every Saturday night Willembrock would ride his horse to the Red Cow and, at three cents a mug, partake freely of the tavern's beer. It appears he was out to prove that beer and beer drinking were Germany's greatest contribution to the world. On one such night, for

The *Die Rotie Kuh*, or The Red Cow Tavern was located at the intersection of Red Run and Fivepointville Roads in Lancaster County. This grand stone farmhouse sits on one corner of that intersection today.

example, he became so drunk that he could not mount his horse to return home without the help of fellow patrons. The young bucks knew the horse would find its way back unaided, and so once the General was mounted, they slapped the animal on the rump and sent it off with a gallop, the General hanging on for dear life.

Being somewhat antic chaps themselves, the pranksters ran ahead to a stone bridge spanning Muddy Creek that they knew the drunken Willembrock would cross on his way home. Covering themselves with white sheets they had brought with them, they hid under the bridge and waited for Willembrock to arrive. When the horse and rider started to cross the bridge, the "ghosts" jumped up in fiendish delight, spooking the horse. As it ran away with its besotted rider, the jokesters could hear the pickled general shouting a string of German oaths into the night.

Locals also enjoyed talking about another local who was known to frequent the Red Cow on a regular basis. Jacob Fry, it was recalled, felt a need to quench his thirst one day while carrying a heavy crate of apples home to his mother. Fry felt he needed to rejuvenate his energy to make the rest of the trip and so he stopped at the tavern and partook liberally of the fare. After teetering out of the tavern on unsteady legs, Fry started down a rutted

AT the intersection of Napierville Road and Landis Road in Lancaster County, a farm field and thick forests now occupy the ground where the quaint village of Noodle Doosie could once be found.

dirt road and fell. Apples were scattered in all directions, and the drunken man hastily tried to retrieve them all. It is not revealed in the tale how Fry's mother reacted or what she said to him when she discovered that some of the apples he had recovered were of the "road apple" or horse variety.[28]

Those who want to find the former village of Noodle Doosie can easily do so. To get to Noodle Doosie, follow Route 322 east from Ephrata and turn right onto Napierville Road. Follow Napierville Road to a "T" intersection with Landis Road. Get out of the car and stand in what was once downtown Noodle Doosie.

Die Rotie Kuh, or The Red Cow Tavern, was located at the intersection of Red Run and Fivepointville Roads. It was still standing thirty-two years ago but is no longer there today.

The Napierville area could also still boast of at least one local antic chap up until 2018. That year Pennsylvania Dutch folk humorist Melvin Horst died. He was a fluent speaker of the Pennsylvania Dutch dialect and when

---

28. Ibid.

At the opposite corner of Red Run and Fivepointville Road today, this too may have been where the Red Cow Tavern once sat.

performing his comedic routine at county fairs and festivals he became the much-loved Jakey Budderschnip of Noodle Doosie.[29]

SLIPPERY ROCK

Located in Slippery Rock Township of Butler County, the town is named after an oil-slickened rock that once could be found in the nearby creek of the same name. Historians indicate that at this spot near a shelf of sandstone, an Indian trail (perhaps a branch of the Logstown Path or the Kuskusky-Venango Path) forded the stream. A natural oil seep made the rock here exceptionally slippery, and it was this landmark that was the basis for the name of the creek. Although the rock is still there, near present-day Armstrong Bridge in McConnell's Mill State Park, the oil that once seeped from the ground was drained away by oil wells that flourished here in the late 1800s. (See the chapter titled "What's in a name?" in the author's *Pennsylvania Fireside Tales Volume 6* for more details).[30]

---

29. http://www.papergreat.com/2018/01/business-card-for-late-jakey.html.
30. https://www.pa.gov/agencies/dcnr/recreation/where-to-go/state-parks/find-a-park/mcconnells-mill-state-park/history.html.

Legend has it that in colonial times, soldiers were being chased by the local Seneca Indians. The troops, wearing heavy boots, were able to cross the creek, but the Indians, wearing moccasins, slipped on the rocks in the creek bed. They named the creek Wechachochapohka—a slippery rock. Some versions of the story have George Washington as the object of the Indians' pursuit, claiming that it was at this rock that George Washington narrowly escaped death by an Indian warrior who was chasing him. Washington managed to safely cross the creek using the slickened rock as a steppingstone, but the warrior lost his footing on the same rock, causing his gun to misfire, thereby sparing the life of the future "Father of our Country."[31]

SNAKE SPRING VALLEY RUN

Located in Snake Spring Township of Bedford County, the origin of the name of the valley through which this small creek flows remains a subject of debate. One tradition is that "the Snake Indians frequented the spring and had a village or camping ground near it."[32] Historians strongly refute this explanation since no Pennsylvania Indian tribe by that name has ever been identified.

Then there is a humorous folklore tale or tall tale that has been brought forth as the true explanation for the valley's name. The basis for it comes from the "wonderful amount of snakes that used to infest the valley." Among the most common variety of those serpents was the rattlesnake, and of those "there was a sort of mongrel rattlesnake that, whenever he heard or discovered anyone near, he would utter a piercing whistle, and in less time than it takes to write this there would be hundreds of snakes on the scene of action, ready for battle."[33]

On the other hand, there is a more convincing and plausible natural explanation for the valley's name. It comes from an 1877 publication of the German Baptist Brethren (later known as Church of the Brethren) where it was written that "before the days of canal boats, railroads, and telegraphs, goods were forwarded from Philadelphia to Pittsburgh, and from there westward, on pack horses . . . and as they passed to and fro along this road they stopped at this spring to water and eat their lunch, and as the place

---

31. Slippery Rock University website at https://www.sru.edu/community/.
32. Waterman and Watkins, *History of Bedford, Somerset, and Fulton Counties Pennsylvania*, 269–70.
33. Author Unknown, "Old Snake Spring," *Bedford Gazette*, Bedford, June 20, 1890.

was infested with snakes . . . received the name Snake Spring." Before long this term was used of the valley itself, so this tradition says."[34]

And so, the list of unusual Pennsylvania place names seems unending. I keep finding more and more of them, and I will continue to compile them. Maybe there's a book in it some day!

---

34. Author Unknown, "Snake Spring Valley," *Primitive Christian,* an early publication of the German Baptist Brethren (later known as Church of the Brethren), 1877.

CHAPTER 9

ODDS AND ENDS

In addition to the many natural landmarks that are included in the Sunbury Press *Pennsylvania Mountain Landmarks* series, there are some other interesting landmarks of historical significance that deserve mention as well, even though they are of the manmade variety. These landmarks often go unnoticed since they are located in out-of-the-way spots or sit along infrequently traveled mountain roadways or trails. Moreover, unless the traveler knows these landmarks are there, they will breeze right by them, oblivious to an interesting historical artifact that lends a nostalgic touch to the landscape. Following are several examples that fall into that category.

WILDCAT ROCK
Local hunter George Oswald just had to show that he had some bragging rights after shooting three wildcats at this rock back in 1946. It must have taken a lot of work to drag all that cement, blocks, bricks and large "tombstone" all the way up the mountain to this remote spot and then assemble it. His creation is located along the Quehanna hiking trail in the Quehanna Wild Area of Moshannon State Forest in Clearfield County. Officially there is only one wild cat in Pennsylvania. Its scientific name is Lynx rufus, but it is commonly known as the wildcat, bobcat, bay lynx, red lynx and swamp tiger.[1]

There may be some wildcats that still visit this same spot even today since the bobcat has not been declared extinct in Pennsylvania. Information

---
1. Commonwealth of Pennsylvania website: https://www.pa.gov/agencies/pgc/wildlife/discover-pa-wildlife/bobcats.html.

Wildcat Rock along the Quehanna hiking trail in the Quehanna Wild Area of Moshannon State Forest in Clearfield County.

about the bobcat on a Pennsylvania Game Commission website notes: "Rarely seen but surprisingly numerous, the bobcat (Lynx rufus) prowls most of Pennsylvania's woods throughout much of the state. Predominantly staying out of sight, when it is seen the bobcat is sometimes mistaken for the common housecat or a mountain lion."[2]

That they were common in Pennsylvania at one time is evidenced by the fact that other areas of the state bear their name as well. Wildcat Creek, a tributary of the Lackawanna River in Lackawanna County, Wildcat Rocks in Michaux State Forest of Adams, Cumberland, and Franklin Counties, and the small village of Wildcat in Madison Township of Clarion County are several examples.

---

2. Ibid.

PANTHER ROCK

This unusual rock sculpture of a mountain lion, known to early settlers as panthers, can be found west of Weedville in Elk County. Sitting about one mile from the intersection of Gardner Hill Road and Byrnedale Road, and then northwest along Gardner Hill Road, it is a unique landmark in Bennett's Valley. Local artist Andy Shutters carved it in 1991, and to this day it serves as a reminder of the area's natural and cultural heritage.

Bennett's Valley was originally a wilderness before the first pioneer settlers arrived here in the last decades of the eighteenth century. Among those first settlers were the Bennetts. John Bennett and his father settled here in 1787, and it is from them that Bennett's Valley was named. Prior to them, the area was a favorite hunting spot for Native American hunters. Wild game of all types abounded, including wolves, panthers, catamounts, elk, and deer. The streams also teemed with aquatic life. One early settler in the Driftwood area, when describing that abundance, claimed that eels were particularly plentiful, and that "he could catch enough fish in twenty minutes to feed his family for a week."[3]

Panther Rock is a unique landmark in Bennett's Valley of Elk County. It serves as a reminder of the area's natural and cultural heritage.

---

3. Webpage of the Mount Zion Historical Society https://mtzionhistoricalsociety.org/history/stories/unique-hunting-camps-of-bennetts-valley/.

Similarly, in the first half of the nineteenth century, mountain lions still roamed these hills. In March of 1853, it is recorded that Erasmus Morey and Peter Smith killed six full grown panthers along Medix Run, the largest measuring thirteen feet from its nose to the tip of its tail. Later in that same year five more of the beasts were shot in the Medix Run area by hunters Bill and Jack Long. Early records in nearby Clearfield County also show that Erasmus Morey was awarded a bounty of $12.00 each for a number of wolves he killed in that county.[4]

Today the natural order in Elk County and its neighboring counties is much different, but elk introduced by the Pennsylvania Game Commission starting in 1913 have flourished again and draw many tourists every year. Wolves no longer can be found here, but the mournful howls of the coyote sometimes echo across the ridges. Also in recent years, there have been some reports of mountain lion sightings throughout the county, but none have been substantiated. Therefore, the panther on that rock sculpture in Bennett's Valley may have to maintain its lonely vigil for some time to come.

THE TICKING TOMBSTONE

On the grounds of the White Clay Creek Nature Preserve in southern Chester County there is a small cemetery with a tombstone that has an unusual story. In the stone-walled cemetery rest many of the first settlers in the area. However, this land was settled long before they came here.

The burial ground sits next to the London Tract Baptist Meetinghouse built in 1729. A historical plaque which provides a brief history of this unique place was placed on a large boulder outside the cemetery by the Pennsylvania Historical Commission and Chester County Historical Society in 1934. The inscription on the plaque states that the church and cemetery grounds were once the site of an Indian town called Minguannan. It also states that the group of Indians living here were of the Lenni Lenape or Delaware Unami Group, that their totem was the tortoise, and that Machaloha or Owhala was the name of their chief. The plaque also reveals that it was this same group who sold to William Penn "the lands between the Delaware River and Chesapeake Bay to the falls of the Susquehanna in 1683."

---

4. Website of the Mount Zion Historical Society https://mtzionhistoricalsociety.org/history/stories/the-elk-panther-and-mountain-lions/.

The cemetery of the ticking tombstone, Located next to the London Tract Baptist Meetinghouse on the grounds of the White Clay Creek Nature Preserve in southern Chester County.

In checking the name of the Indian town mentioned on the plaque, I find no mention of it in Donehoo's *Indian Villages and Place Names in Pennsylvania*. Likewise. I do not find the name of the plaque's Indian chief in Sipe's *Indian Chiefs of Pennsylvania*. Moreover, in searching through Futhey and Cope's *History of Chester County* (particularly under the chapter titled "Proprietary Interests and Land Titles") there are references to land purchases from the Indians, but nothing about the 1683 purchase recorded on the plaque.

Perhaps the historical society had sources of their own confirming the plaque's details, but lack of historical documentation that confirms the plaque details today also throws some doubt on the legend that is told about the curious tombstone in the church cemetery. As can be seen from its picture, it qualifies as a true "landmark," lying flat on the surface of the land around it and decorating that landscape with a macabre impression. But to the legend.

There are two versions of the tale, one that dates back to the time (1763–1767) when Charles Mason and Jeremiah Dixon were tasked to survey the boundary line separating Maryland and Pennsylvania. There

A view of tombstones in the cemetery of the ticking tombstone.

was a dispute about that boundary between the Calverts of Maryland and the Penns of Pennsylvania which was finally resolved when the official Mason/Dixon Line was laid out. That borderline also became historically significant during the Civil War when it was a demarcation between free and slave states, and also the basis for the term "Dixie."[5]

Apparently Jeremiah Dixon, according to the first account, always carried an ornate pocket watch which somehow ended up in the hands of one of his workers. When he died, the worker asked to be buried with that watch. Shortly thereafter there were those who, when visiting his grave, swore they could hear the watch ticking away if they put their ear to the tombstone.

The second account claimed that Dixon's pocket watch ended up in the hands, and stomach, of another individual. In this tall tale it's related that one day a small infant named Fithian Minuet crawled into the surveyor's tent, attracted by the shiny objects stored inside. The baby was quite the voracious tot since it was known for trying to swallow anything it picked up. On this day he could not resist Dixon's fancy pocket watch, popped it into his mouth, and managed to swallow it. There it remained, ticking away, for the rest of his life. That's why, perhaps, he became a clockmaker.

---

5. https://www.history.com/news/why-is-the-south-known-as-dixie.

A tombstone with an unusual epitaph in the cemetery of the ticking tombstone.

Closeup of that tombstone with the unusual epitaph in the cemetery of the ticking tombstone.

The Infamous Ticking Tombstone

He worked in a shop filled with the sound of ticking clocks, which masked the clicking of the one inside him.

The amazing timepiece, so says the legend, continued to tick, even after Minuit was buried in the same cemetery where his beloved wife was interred before him. The ticking, it was said, would go on eternally, thereby symbolizing the eternal love the couple had for one another, just as they hoped it would.[6]

This last tale, of course, is at best one of the taller ones that can be heard anywhere. Not only is it not likely that a young baby could swallow a pocket watch, but it is even less likely that a pocket watch, which requires winding on a daily basis, would continue to tick ad infinitum. Such fantasy is dismissed by rational folks today, and when I was directed to the tombstone by the park's ranger and asked him about the ticking sounds, he said there "never was any ticking" and it just made for a good story.

The park has another legendary figure who might be upset by such a dismissive attitude, or at least that's what those who believe in her might feel. There have been reports by some that they have on occasion seen the ghostly figure of an Indian maiden floating around the tombstones in the cemetery. Perhaps she's unable to find peace because there are no longer

6. Steven Hoffman, "The Mystery of the Ticking Tomb—Examining Famous Local Legend Near: Landenberg," *Chester County Press,* October 19, 2020.

Closeup of the infamous Ticking Tombstone with its RC initials. No ticking to be heard here!

vestiges of her village that once stood on this site, or maybe she too is grounded to this spot by an eternal love that knows no end.

ENGINE ROCK

Those traveling along Devil's Elbow Road west of the small village of Yarnall in Boggs Township of Centre County undoubtedly proceed with a degree of caution at times, given the suggestive nature of the road's name. There is no supernatural legend or tale that is the basis for the name, but there is an exceedingly sharp curve in the road at one point which is devilishly hard to navigate if a driver does not slow down.

Travel over the heights of the Bald Eagle Mountain range north of Yarnall was always a steep and arduous journey, especially in the days of the earliest settlements here. As one historian noted in 1883, "Much of

Plaque at the London Tract Baptist Church Cemetery that preserves the memory of the Indian town called *Minguannan* that once stood here and of Machaloha the name of their chief.

the territory is rough and a great deal of it mountainous, and much yet a stranger to the plow of the husbandman."[7]

Life in the earliest days in Nittany Valley was rough also, as Andrew Walker was to find out after clearing some land and building his log cabin at the base of the mountain. He was one of the first settlers here, and he had to share his little place in the wilderness with wolves and panthers, which "were thick and bold enough to come even to Walker's cabin door."[8]

It must have been an extremely harrowing experience for Walker's wife and their four children since "the cabin door was indeed at first not a very

---

7. John Blair Linn, *History of Centre and Clinton Counties*, 260–63.
8. Ibid.

substantial affair, since it consisted of a bed-quilt hung over the opening left for a door, and similarly the windows were sheets."[9] Moreover, the nearest neighbors were in the valley below, and so the family had to endure a forlorn life of isolation.

The fields and forests along the aforementioned Devil's Elbow Road are still sparsely settled, and the rough terrain slows traffic down a bit, just like it did back in the Walkers' era. It is a delay that probably sometimes irritates those who are in a hurry to get where they are going, but for those traveling along Devil's Elbow Road and then taking a side mountain road off to the west, it may be a blessing in disguise. The reason for that seemingly unfounded remark is that when travelers slow down, they may catch a glimpse of an unusual engraving on a large rock sitting on the side of the roadway.

The anonymous artist who carved the image, of a railroad engine towing a train car behind it, onto the rock was very meticulous in his work. There is a cloud of smoke billowing out the smokestack of the engine, wheels and windows of the engine and the car it is towing are clearly visible, as is the cowcatcher at the front of the engine. To this day no one has claimed the credit as the rock's engraver, nor has anyone claimed to know who the engraver was. Whoever it was, they must have been a big fan of trains, and of one local railroad in particular; one whose lines followed the course of the Bald Eagle Creek in Nittany Valley.

When the financially troubled Tyrone and Lock Haven Railroad was bailed out by the powerful Pennsylvania Railroad (PRR) in 1861, it became the Bald Eagle Valley Railroad. Subsequent extensions of its lines included branch lines into the Snowshoe coal regions and one from Bellefonte into Lemont. Then in 1892 the Bellefonte Central made a connection with the PRR line at Lemont.[10]

It was a longed-for update welcomed by students trying to get to the original Farmer's High School (established in 1855), but by then known as the Pennsylvania State College (which would be renamed again in 1953, becoming the Pennsylvania State University). Prior to the new Bellefonte Central connection, students coming from Philadelphia, Pittsburgh, and other distant cities had to take a train to Lewistown or Spruce Creek and

---

9. Ibid.
10. Details found throughout: Thomas T. Taber III, *Railroads of Pennsylvania Encyclopedia and Atlas*; and Christopher T. Baer, *A General Chronology of the Pennsylvania Railroad Company Predecessors and Successors and its Historical Context*.

Engine Rock along Devil's Elbow Road west of the small village of Yarnall in Boggs Township of Centre County. It commemorates the days of the steam trains which hauled coal and lumber during the area's industrial heydey.

then make an additional day's long stagecoach ride to State College. The trip was now shorter, but it still seemed to many that the Pennsylvania State College was still a remote place.

As Edwin Sparks, president of Penn State from 1908 to 1920, would say during his tenure, the college was "Equally inaccessible from all parts of the state."[11]

It was true that those riding the rails into State College during President Spark's tenure usually had to change trains several times to get there. Moreover, both the PRR and Bellefonte Central Railroad (BCR) branches were "rail backwaters," characterized by slow trains and passenger service that was far from first class.

Consequently, the eighteen-mile train trips between Bellefonte and State College often took an hour and a quarter. Nonetheless, the leisurely journey allowed passengers to enjoy the pastoral scenery along the way. The trips also led to fond BCR memories often recalled by Penn State faculty and students, including those about Ross Parker, its senior conductor. Students in that day referred to the BCR as "Parker's Boat,"[12] since the train had once been caught in a flash flood. But it was another tale about Parker

---

11. https://libraries.psu.edu/about/collections/penn-state-university-park-campus-history-collection/penn-state-illustrated-15.
12. Ibid.

that Penn State professor Fred Lewis Pattee liked to recall, and which has been preserved in the Penn State Archives.

As Pattee would relate, there was a trainload of undergraduates who, having completed their final exams, were anxious to get back home for the holidays. At some point on the way, the train came to an unexpected stop. This did not set well with the students, and one of the more impatient ones shouted out "Hey Parker, what are you stopping the train for?"

"Calves on the track," came the calm reply from the conductor. "Got to shoo them off!"

Then in about half an hour, the train came to another unscheduled stop. Once again, an impatient passenger shouted out to Parker, "Say Parker, what are we stopping for again?"

"Those damn calves have got back on the track again," explained Parker, and the passengers had to sit tight while those "damn calves" were shooed off the track.[13]

Perhaps it was memories like this that inspired an artist to engrave the likeness of a railroad engine on engine rock along Devil's Elbow Road. On the other hand, some might say, in a tongue in cheek sort of way and as the old saying goes, "the devil made him do it!"

GHOST ROCK

The area known as the Scotia Barrens in Centre County is well known to lovers of nature and to conservationists who tirelessly work to protect the state's natural areas. Once the site of a thriving iron ore industry, large chunks of "The Barrens" or the "Pine Barrens," as it is referred to locally, have been preserved in a natural state thanks to philanthropists who have purchased them and set them aside as a game refuge.

For some years I lived in Halfmoon Valley just next to the Barrens and, as a member of the Halfmoon Valley Open Space Preservation Board, helped to conserve some of the valley's beautiful fields and farms. In the years I lived there I also collected and preserved some of the local legends and folktales that could once be heard about the Barrens and the area around it. For some of them see the author's *Pennsylvania Fireside Tales Volume 2 (The Black Ghost of Scotia and More Pennsylvania Fireside Tales)*, the chapter titled "Stretching It" in *Pennsylvania Fireside Tales Volume 5*, the chapter titled "Give Me the Good Old Days" in *Pennsylvania Fireside*

---
13. Ibid.

Along Marengo Road that leads to the Scotia Barrens Country and past "Spooky Hollow". It was along here, and perhaps at this very spot, where the "Ghost Rock" could be seen, and, on nights of a full moon where the image of the dancing Indian princess was seen by a select few.

Tales Volume 6, and the chapter titled "Warriors' Mark" in *Pennsylvania Mountain Landmarks Volume 1*.

And much to my delight, I continue to discover and to be told more tales of the same area. Just recently, for example, one of my Preservation Board friends told me about a place once called "Spooky Hollow" just outside Warriors Mark in Huntingdon County. I had asked my friend if he knew about a place of that name along Marengo Road near Pennsylvania Furnace on the Centre/Huntingdon County line, but he knew nothing about it. He did know of one such place, however, but it was just not the one I had asked about.

This other dark and mysterious place was located along Route 550 where the Warriors Mark fire hall sits today. My friend recalled that in his youth he and his friends, on their bicycle rides, would pedal their bikes as fast as they could when going through what was then a dark and uninviting section of woodland. Fearful of its reputation as a place where ghosts dwelt, the boys would ride as fast as possible down the road leading through the hollow so they could get enough momentum to climb the road leading up and out of it.[14]

The Spooky Hollow I had asked about was, like the Warriors Mark hollow of the same name, in its day also considered to be the home of

---
14. Lee Pressler, interviewed August 3, 2024.

ghosts—more accurately the abode of a single ghost. As such it was a place that locals avoided, especially when passing through here after darkness had fallen. They did not want to encounter the ghost that many had claimed to have seen here. Witnesses talked of a large flat rock lying along the roadside north of what used to be Rider's Dam, and on it they claimed to have seen a spectral image of a young Indian maiden swaying and dancing in luminescent moonlight mists.

The dam is still there today, but despite my efforts to locate the flat rock in question, I could not find it. My friend, who had grown up here, knew of no such rock either, or of a place called Spooky Hollow along Marengo Road. Heavy lumbering operations and erections of many houses along the road over the decades have obviously destroyed, turned over, or covered over the flat rock that served as a dance floor for the spectral Indian maid.

I found several flat rocks that lie along the roadside today (see photos), but none of them seemed large enough or flat enough to fit the rock described in the legend of the dancing maiden's ghost. The legend was recalled by Dr. W. Frank Beck, a highly regarded medical doctor of Altoona, who was born in Loveville, Halfmoon Township, in 1866, dying at age 79 in 1945.

According to Dr. Beck, who was also regarded as a "veteran historian,"[15] it was a story he often heard from his aunts and uncles, who, he recalled, all believed in ghosts. As a young lad, it left a strong impression upon him, and he said that even though he and his friends never believed there was a ghost dancing on the rock, it was the reason they always avoided it at night. Dr. Beck, for instance, said he recalled passing it only once at night "but never the second time!"[16]

Spooky Hollow in his day "was a meek and lazy place, beautiful and too good to be true." There was "no other place like it," he asserted, and "it makes you believe something unusual might happen there, especially when it's real dark. And many people that have visited Spooky Hollow with me have come away with that same feeling."[17]

He then went on to tell the story of the ghost rock. The story "runs back to the Indian days," he claimed, "and it was from them that this rock derived its name. It is a long and curious story," he went on, and it

---

15. Doctor William F. Beck, *History of the Beck Family and Their Descendants Everywhere Including Bucks, Graziers, Nearfhoofs and Kriders. The Pioneer Settlers of Warriors Mark Valley, 1768 to 1940.*
16. Doctor W. Frank Beck, "Ghosts of the Barrens," *Altoona Tribune*, April 30, 1943.
17. Ibid.

A view of Rider's Dam along Marengo Road. It is still there today, and nearby there was a dark depression in the woods locals called Spooky Hollow with its ghost rock. Neither the hollow nor the ghost rock seem to exist anymore; both apparently lost to lumberng operations, highway expansion, and housing developments.

occurred "back in the days when the unhappy Indians of the Pine Barrens, surrounded and harassed by the whites, were on their way out."

The story culminated, he would state, when "A heartbroken old chief decided to have his daughter fast for ten days, then dance the ghost dance on the rock." The chief maintained, Beck explained, that if she was to continue this dancing for the full ten days, it would induce their great spirit to give them a great victory over the white interlopers and drive them out. But the chief's wise man protested, saying the Indians' fate was destined to end elsewhere and so their god's will was not to be contested.

The wise man's entreaties fell on deaf ears, and the chief forced his daughter to fast for the full ten days, allowing her to partake of neither food nor water the whole time. After surviving this ordeal, she was so weak that she had to be helped up onto the rock to begin her dancing on a moonlit night. Dr. Beck would then conclude his story, saying "She had hardly taken a step when she fell down in a heap dead."

It is her spirit, he would then say, that is sometimes seen dancing upon the ghost rock on nights of a full moon, and which is also often seen on moonlit nights floating amongst the vaporous mists shimmering in the dark shadows of the Barrens.[18]

---

18. Ibid.

Lonely Grave of the CCC worker along Sand Mountain Road which leads back to Poe Valley State Park.

A LONELY GRAVE

Nestled on a hillside along the mountain road leading back to Poe Valley and Poe Paddy State Parks, is a little-noticed gravestone. An inscription on its metal plaque reads "In Memory of Bernard Oyler, Asst. Leader, C. C. C. Co. 1333, Killed In Line of Duty, Jan. 25, 1935".

Few people recall the full story behind Oyler's tragic death and lonely grave, but the current owner of the property on which the memorial is located, shared those details with my wife and I one fine summer day when we stopped to make inquiries. He happened to be at his hunting camp and was happy to share the story as it had been told to him.

Apparently the unlucky CCC worker was hit by a falling tree when he was helping to clear the area for the CCC camp. It was wintertime and when the tree hit him, it buried his head in a snowbank. It was believed that he did not die by being crushed by the tree, but from being suffocated in the deep snow. When his parents were notified, they asked the CCC camp to bury him where he had fallen since they could not afford to ship his body back home. Whether they were able to eventually visit their son's gravesite or not, is anyone's guess. In any case, his last resting place remains a lonely and forlorn spot and a bleak reminder of the dangers faced by those tireless CCC workers in Pennsylvania's forests.[19]

---

19. Yarnall, Jack, interviewed 06/13/2010.

CHAPTER 10

NATIVE AMERICAN EPITAPHS

I have always been fascinated and intrigued by geographical Pennsylvania place names that start with the word Indian. The words make me wonder what history lies behind those titles; what stories do they hide behind those curious appellations? Moreover, it seems that in a sense they may serve as a kind of epitaph for the Native Americans who inspired locals to memorialize them in that way. In this chapter we will explore some of those Indian names and attempt to discover the mysteries they hold.

INDIAN GRAVE RUN/INDIAN GRAVE ROAD (Fulton County)

Surely there had to be some interesting history associated with these interesting places in Fulton County, and diligent search proved that this is indeed the case. The stream and roadway with these names can be found in Buck Valley of that county, near the village of Amaranth just west of Route 70. The dale, originally called Whipper Cove, is a picturesque region, described by one historian as a "true upland valley, surrounded by mountains and abounding in countless springs of pure, wholesome water." And as if that were not enough praise to heap upon the place, the historian also noted that "the mountain scenery is beautiful, and it is considered one of the handsomest valleys in the state for its size."[1]

---

1. Waterman and Watkins, *History of Bedford, Somerset and Fulton Counties, Pennsylvania*, 665–66.

The scenic upland can also boast of a dramatic history, dating back to the times when the first settler came here in 1795. Those colonists not only had to contend with the rigors of frontier life but also had to deal with threats of Indian invasions during the times fraught with border warfare. At that time, what is now Fulton County was, until formed as a separate county in 1850, still part of Bedford County. During the perilous times of the French and Indian War in the 1750s, the settlers in this area were regularly killed, scalped, and carried away as captives by Native American war parties.

The hardy pioneers gave as good as they got at times, and it is from one of these battles, so history tells us, that the name Indian Grave Run got its name. The skirmish is mentioned briefly in an early history of Fulton County where it says that "Indian Grave Run was named from an Indian buried there. He was killed by Abner Hunt and Emanual Smith, who followed them, the Indian in company with others, from Potomac River. Hunt and Emanual Smith were captured while following the Indian at Bald Hill, on the Alleghenies."[2]

No mention of this event seems to be recorded in any other histories of the area, including Sipe's *Indian Wars* or Loudon's *Narratives*. We are therefore left to ponder when it happened and whether it is even a recollection of an actual episode or not. History does record that in 1755 "more than 30 persons were killed and scalped or taken captive within 30 days near the Bedford County line in Maryland."[3]

To shed further light on the Indian Grave Run incident, it may prove interesting to present a narrative about a similar episode that occurred during the mid-1750s in what was still Bedford County at that time. If nothing else, it does show that lone Indians were sometimes shot by early settlers of that county and that the dead men were interred where they had fallen.

"John Perrin's first wife was a sister of John Ray. She was captured at the same time as Mrs. Vogan, Mrs. Clark, Mrs. Davis, and Mrs. Tombleson. This Indian raid was made by the Shawnee chief Wills. After traveling some three miles, Mrs. Perrin was unable to keep up with the fleeing Indians. On the point of Tussey's mountain, near two white rocks, known as Perrin's Rocks, she was killed and scalped with her infant baby. The alarm being

---

2. Ibid.
3. William P. Schell, *Annals of Bedford County*, 6.

given, the Indians and their captives were pursued by Perrin, Davis, Vogan, Clark, George and Joseph Powell, and Michael Huff.

"These men came up with the Indians on the top of Wills Mountain. They found that the captors of the women had been joined by about one hundred other savages. The pursuers hoped that during the night they would be able to release the captives. When morning came, the Indians held a counsel, when about seventy-five of them with the captives started west, with the others going north, except Chief Wills who remained at the camping place until late evening when he also left camp and was carefully followed. At dark they discovered a small light at the very pinnacle of Wills knob.

"Cautiously approaching, George Powell discovered the Indian alone and in a sitting position. Powell was up-on the alert and at the distance of seventy steps; when his firelock rang over the still mountain range, the old chief's spirit took its flight to the Happy Hunting Ground. His "topknot" was removed, his grave dug, and his body laid therein. The body was removed about the year 1825 by unknown parties. The grave is still there and will be till time is no more. Any person that is skeptical as to this fact can visit this spot and see for himself, as your correspondent has done. The surviving women were found at Montreal, Canada, and brought home some six years afterward."[4]

COMMENTS:

1. The gravesite of Chief Wills was on top of Wills Mountain, less than two miles west of present-day Bedford and a short distance from the Jean Bonnet Tavern.[5]
2. The locations of the Indian Grave Run and Wills Mountain incidents, although occurring in adjacent counties, were still widely separated geographically. Indian Grave run is located near the western edge of Fulton County, while Wills Mountain lies at the western edge of Bedford County.
3. Given the separation mentioned in the previous comment, the pursuers following the captors of Mrs. Perrin would have faced some

---

4. John H. P. Adams, Esquire, "Early Local History," *The Bedford Gazette*, March 29, 1907, 3.
5. Regina Williams, *History of Southampton Township*, October 20, 2009. http://southamptonhistory.blogspot.com/.

formidable heights along the way. Before reaching Wills Mountain, they would have had to climb over Warrior Ridge, Tussey Mountain, Martin Mountain, Evitts Mountain, and Shriver Ridge, not to mention some minor ridges along the way. Quite a testament to the physical stamina the men of that age must have had!

INDIAN LANE (Centre County)

This dirt lane leading back to an active farmstead was named to commemorate a battle between five Indians and two soldiers who may have been guarding reapers in the field that still adjoins the lane on its western side. Along this same side is a monument marking the spot where the soldiers are believed to have been buried, following their murder at the hands of five warriors who invaded the area in July 1778. The two troopers were stationed at the Upper or Potter's Fort in Penns Valley, one of the three frontier forts erected here during the Revolutionary War. The story of the battle that took place along Indian Lane, and more information about the monument that still sits along the roadside, can be found in Chapter 11

Indian Lane, Potter Township, Centre County. The adjoining field is where two soldiers from Potter's Fort were killed in a fight with five warriors.

The Indian Lane Monument, dedicated in memory of the two soldiers who died here defending reapers in the adjoining field.

titled "Burned at the Stake" in the second volume of the author's *Pennsylvania Fireside Tales*.

An interesting sequel to the story was provided by preeminent historian John Blair Linn in a letter dated November 4, 1872. In that letter, Linn describes the hand-to-hand battle that took place at this spot in 1778 and adds a different twist to the claim that the soldiers who were attacked by the Indians were there guarding reapers harvesting their crops. Instead, Linn notes, "I have little to add to the above except the tradition in the neighborhood is that the soldiers went out to hunt wild turkeys and were lured by imitated turkey calls of the Indians, a trick that became too common to deceive the settlers afterwards.

"I am indebted to my uncle, Dr. William I. Wilson of Potter's Mills for the following sequel to the story. He told me, a few days since, that quite a number of years after the occurrence, Hon. Andrew Gregg (the elder) came along the road and stopped to have a chat with James Alexander, who then farmed the whole of the fort farm. Alexander had a nervous

Close up of the inscription on the Indian Lane Monument.

habit when standing talking, of kicking up the ground about him, and while conversing with Mr. Gregg he kept kicking as usual, and on the spot uncovered a large hunting knife, which from its rusted condition and general appearance, indicated that it had lain there ever since the conflict, and was undoubtedly either the knife of the soldier or of the Indian killed. Two stones were procured and set upon the spot, in memory of the two soldiers who sold their lives so dearly there. The farm was afterwards divided up, and it was on that part of it now owned by William Henney. I should be glad to hear that someone has been successful in finding the spot."[6]

A large monument replacing the two stones marking the spot was placed there in 1900 by the local chapter of the Daughters of the American Revolution (see photo). They did so in the belief that the two soldiers who lost

---

6. John Blair Linn, letter dated November 4, 1872, appearing in an article titled "Revolutionary Incident," *Centre Democrat*, Bellefonte, Pennsylvania, November 8, 1872.

their lives in the battle with the five Indians here were buried where they had fallen—the place where James Alexander uncovered the rusty knife. Whether the soldiers were here guarding reapers or not, cannot be ascertained from the earliest account of the episode which is found in Linn's *History of Centre and Clinton Counties,* where he quotes a letter written by General Potter from his fort (the upper fort in Penn's Valley) on July 25, 1778.

In writing about the event Potter begins by noting "Yesterday two men of Capt. Finley's company of Col. Brodhead's regiment, went out from this place on the plains a little below my fields, and met a party of Indians, five in number, who they engaged."[7]

Linn's sequel of November 4, 1872, would indicate that the two soldiers were not guarding reapers when attacked by the band of warriors, but instead may have indeed just gone out of the fort to do nothing more than to perhaps merely amuse themselves by hunting wild turkeys. If so, then it is not surprising that they were lured to their deaths by the Indians' imitated wild turkey calls.

INDIAN GRAVE HILL/INDIAN GRAVE ROAD (Centre County)

As the name implies, this small mountain knoll near the town of Snow Shoe, in Snow Shoe Township of Centre County, must be the last resting place of a local Native American. If so, then his gravesite must be here somewhere, perhaps marked at least by a mound of stone or a single upright rectangular unmarked rock. However, this does not seem to be the case. The burial site has been lost in the mists of time. My queries about it to locals who have lived on Indian Grave Hill for over fifty years led to dead ends (no pun intended) as to the whereabouts of the gravesite and any stories about it.

Moreover, when surveying the hill one fine March morning in 2025 when the woods were bare and covered with a light skiff of snow, I could see no evidence of any mounds or markers that might reveal a place of interment. The long shadows of the bare trees cast by the sun upon the roadway that day just added to the sense of mystery that pervades this spot. (Please note, this is private property and should be treated as such. I am indebted to the current residents for being so gracious in allowing me to take photos and to ask them questions.)

---

7. John Blair Linn, *History of Centre and Clinton Counties, Pennsylvania,* 20.

On Indian Grave Hill. Located in Snow Shoe Township of Centre County. Its name is supposedly derived from the belief that at this high point on the wooded knoll is the last resting place of a local Native American.

History does shed some light on the matter, however. Early records indicate that not only was there once an Indian camp at the nearby town of Snow Shoe, but also that a heavily used Indian path passed through that same town. In addition, the famous "nest" or village of the great Delaware Lenape chief Woapalanne, or Bald Eagle, was located at the nearby town of Milesburg.

A Pennsylvania Museum and Historical Commission sign at Milesburg serves as a reminder that Bald Eagle's village once flourished here, and in Paul A. W. Wallace's *Indian Paths of Pennsylvania*, we find that The Great Shamokin Path passed through present-day Snow Shoe, coming from the Indian town of Shamokin at the forks of the Susquehanna (present day Sunbury) and on to the Indian town of Kittanning. It must have been a well-traveled pathway since it led from what was, up until the time of the French and Indian War, "the most important Indian town in the province of Pennsylvania" westward to what was at the same time "the largest Indian settlement in Pennsylvania west of Shamokin."[8] Wallace also shows that there were two other important Indian paths that passed through this same section: Bald Eagle's Path and the Bald Eagle Creek Path.[9]

---

8. Paul A. W. Wallace, *Indian Paths of Pennsylvania*, 66.
9. Ibid, 22.

View of the woods on Indian Grave Hill. No burial places to be found here or in any other spots on the hillside.

In conclusion, then, it appears that since many Native Americans lived near and traveled by Indian Grave Hill on a regular basis, it would not be surprising that one or more of them were interred at this spot. Whether or not such an internment will ever be discovered is doubtful, but not outside the realm of the possible. For instance, residents of Sunbury were shocked in 1910 "When in digging a cellar for a new house in Sunbury, workmen ran into an old Indian grave about five feet under the ground. It contained the antlers of a deer, the head of a bear and a number of articles of pottery."[10]

INDIAN HILL (Centre County)

This is yet another site where details about the basis for the name have been forgotten over time. Once again, I inquired of residents about why this area has a Native American designation, and none of them had any idea as to why this is so. It is interesting to note, however, that the field along the right side of the road leading to the development on the hillside has never been developed; the plot remains uncultivated and in a natural state. The reason for it being left untouched would seem to be because it is hallowed

---

10. Francis Speer, "An Indian Grave," *The Centre Democrat*, Bellefonte, Pennsylvania, September 1, 1910.

ground. Those in local governmental positions do appear to realize that this is the case since the following quote about it was included in a 1996 official survey of Centre County cemeteries: "This field is supposedly a large Native American graveyard. It is about 500 x 500 feet and might contain the graves of about 200 Indians." I find no other reference to it in any other local histories.[11]

INDIAN HANNA MONUMENT (Chester County)

A chapter on Indian epitaphs would not be complete without mention of this iconic memorial that sits on the grounds of the Longwood Meeting House, just inside the main entrance to Longwood Gardens in Chester County. Originally dedicated on September 5, 1925, the large granite boulder with a bronze tablet was rededicated on May 15, 2024. The inscription on the tablet reads:

Indian Hannah
1730–1802
the last of the Indians
in Chester County
was born in the vale
about 300 yards to the east
on the land
of the protector of her people,
the Quaker Assemblyman
Willam Webb.
Her mother was Indian Sarah,
and her grandmother was Indian Jane
of the Unami Group,
their totem the tortoise
of the Lenni-Lenape or Delaware Indians
—

Marked by the Pennsylvania Historical Commission and
the Chester County Historical Society in 1925.

---

11. Centre County PAGen Web Project, "Centre County Cemeteries—Indian Graves," https://centre.pagenweb.org/graves.htm.

Also remembered in local legend and lore, Indian Hannah was considered to be the last Lenni Lenape Indian living in Chester County at the time of her death. Moreover, a record of her life was recorded by the overseer of the poor at the Chester County Poorhouse where she spent her last years. She supported herself prior to that time as a domestic servant, working for board in several Quaker homes, and also earned a modest income by selling baskets and brooms she had made herself. Her life story, as recorded by the overseer at the poorhouse, is a remarkable first-person account of what the life of an unmarried poor working woman was like in eighteenth century rural Pennsylvania.[12]

Although Indian Hannah's life story may serve as a reminder of just how the Native American lifestyle was impacted by the unstoppable waves of European immigrants who pushed westward into aboriginal territory during her lifetime, she could not claim the dubious distinction of being the last Native American in Chester County. The Lenni Lenape were not eradicated that easily, and even today their descendants still reside in what was once their traditional homeland in parts of what is now Pennsylvania, Delaware, New Jersey, and Maryland. They continue to proudly uphold the traditions of their race and to fight for some of the lands that they hold so dear. See chapter 12 ("Indian Peg") in the author's *Pennsylvania Fireside Tales Volume 6* for Indian Hanna's story.

OTHER SACRED NATIVE AMERICAN PLACES OF NOTE (Various Counties):

1. Indian Head: The village of this name sits alongside the eastern bank and headwaters of Indian Creek in Fayette County. One explanation for its title claims it is named after the creek that runs next to it. On the other hand, there are those who say it is named from a nearby rock formation that resembles a Native American's head. If there was such a head at one time, it seems to have disappeared, since locals don't seem to know where it is today. Moreover, those same locals wonder why the formation was thought to be the likeness of a Native American since it would have been hard to differentiate it from that of a non-Native American.

---

12. *Blog of the Pennsylvania State Historic Preservation Office*: https://pahistoricpreservation.com/remembering-indian-hannah/

2. Towanda: According to Donehoo in his *Indian Place Names*, the town of this name in Tioga County is named after the creek of the same name. That name is derived from the Indian word *Tawundeunk*, meaning "where we bury the dead." The Munsee Indian village of *Tawandaemenk* stood on the flats at the mouth of the creek.[13]

3. Moravian Indian Grave Yard: Located near the first Moravian graveyard at Nazareth, Northampton County, it was memorialized when a monument of American marble was placed here and dedicated by the Moravian Historical Society in 1867. On the monument there is a plaque that reads in part: "This is the site of the first Moravian graveyard, called "God's Acre," in use from 1744 to 1762. Erroneously thought to be the burial ground of the Indians from the nearby village of Welagamika, there are actually only four Indians buried here." Nearby is another monument called the Indian Graveyard Monument, on which are inscribed the names of 67 Moravians, as well as the names of the four Indians, who are buried here, including "Beata Indian, Died Aug 12 1744 and Sarah Indian born 1740 Died Aug 22 1748."[14]

4. Indian Burial Ground: There is yet another place, this one in Bradford County, where Native Americans laid their loved ones to rest. According to a reputable local historian, "There was an Indian settlement at Luther's Mills and maize was grown on the flats there. The Indians did much hunting and fishing in that locality and an Indian burial ground occupied the exact site of our present County Home."[15]

5. Salisbury Church Graveyard: This awe-inspiring burial spot was once regarded as a place of evil by locals who knew its ghastly tale. See chapter number 7 titled "Panther Days and Nights" in the author's *Pennsylvania Fireside Tales Volume 1* for that story. In this same hallowed ground can be found the final resting place of some Delaware Indians (see photo).

---

13. Doctor George P. Donehoo, *Indian Villages and Place Names in Pennsylvania*, 232.
14. Historical Marker Database at https://www.hmdb.org/m.asp?m=195058.
15. Joyce M. Tice, "Cedar Ledge Monument," *Tri-Counties Genealogy and History*, https://www.joycetice.com/articles/cedarled.htm.

Monument in the Salisbury Church Graveyard, near Emmaus, Lehigh County, dedicated to the memory of the Delaware Indians buried here.

6. Shawana's Grave: I include this gravesite with some caution since it was first brought to the public's attention by Henry W. Shoemaker, whose penchant for inventing and changing history to suit his own agenda has made his many historical claims suspect. Nonetheless, on this site (along Nichols Run Road north of Jersey Shore) can be found a small monument that reads as follows:

SHAWANA
Daughter of Old Nichols A Friendly Seneca
The Last Indian Girl in the West Branch Valley
Died Feb 1855 Aged 16 Years
Erected by the Fort Antes Chapter D. A. R. and
Col. Henry H. Shoemaker

The inscription itself contains at least one error in that Shoemaker's middle initial was not H. (as engraved on the tombstone) but W. In his

Shawana's Grave in the West Branch Valley. Located along Nichols Run Road north of Jersey Shore, Lycoming County.

Eldorado Found volume (page 70), Shoemaker writes that his source for the information about Shawana was John F. Knepley, a "great authority on Indian Lore." He also describes how this site looked prior to the erection of the monument.

In a subsequent 1915 newspaper article he notes, "Last week a party which included John G. Knepley, the gifted pupil of Ole Bull, and John H. Chatham, the sweet singing bard of Central Pennsylvania, visited Shawana's grave. With reverent hands they set up again her fallen tombstone only a bit of mountain brownstone, pulled away the weeds on the mound, and departed."[16]

The description of a single mound with a single upright marker of mountain brownstone seems consistent with Native American burial rituals as described by Count Nikolaus Ludwig Zinzendorf, founder of the Moravian religious sect. Upon visiting the Indian village of Ostonwakin, present day Montoursville, near the mouth of Loyalsock Creek, Lycoming County, in October 1742, he recalled being awakened one morning by the

---

16. Henry W. Shoemaker, "Shawana's Grave," *Altoona Tribune*, 1915 (exact date unknown).

Close up of Shawana's gravesite

sounds of a woman wailing over the grave of her husband. The incident was poignant enough that the Count noted it in the diary he kept throughout his forty years of missionary work among the Indians. It was this incident that also prompted him to record a notation concerning the burial customs of the Indians as far as their practice of erecting "either a stone or a mound in honor of their deceased heroes."[17]

[See also chapter 6 titled "King Widaagh" in the author's *Pennsylvania Mountain Landmarks Volume 2,* for a picture of the vertical gravestone marking the grave of this Indian chief, along Antes Creek near Antes Fort in Lycoming County.]

In my search for additional historical truths behind the Shawana monument's epitaph, I tried to verify whether the names Old Nichols and Shawana were mentioned in any local histories. Consulting many histories of the area, I found no references to any Indians named Old Nichols, but did finally find a reference to a Shawana, but not the one I was looking for. John F. Meginness, one of the most trusted historians of that era, mentions an Indian chief called Shawana Ben. A brief mention of the chief is found

---

17. John F. Meginness, *Otzinachson*, 104.

Close up of the Inscription on Shawana's gravestone

on page 299 of Meginness' *Otzinachson, A History of the West Branch Valley*. However, more detailed information about Shawana Ben is documented in Meginness' *Historical Journal* as follows:

"The Indians, after the destruction of their towns, ceased to congregate in large numbers. All the land west of Lycoming Creek, and north of the river, including the [Great] Island, belonged to the Indians; and it remained in their possession until it was purchased at the treaty of Fort Stanwix in 1784. South of the river the land belonged to the Province of Pennsylvania, having been acquired at the treaty of 1768. In this year Shawana Ben, a friendly Indian, and *Ne-wah-lee-ka*, a Muncy chief of some prominence, were living on the Island.

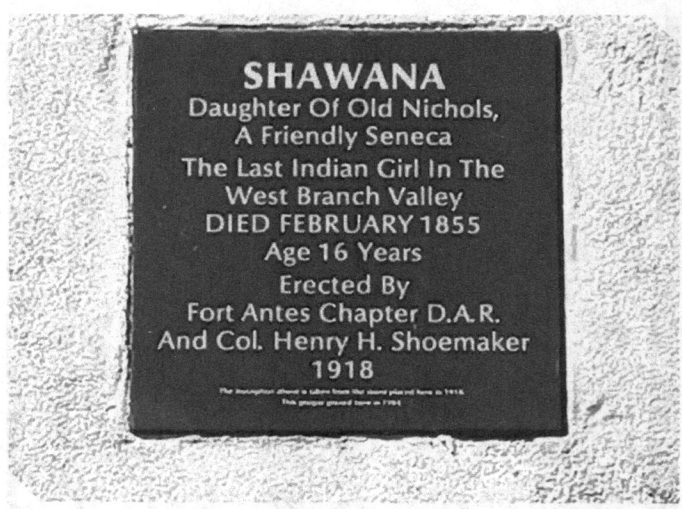

Close up of the historical plaque on Shawana's gravestone

It was called *Mecheck-Menatey* by the Delaware Indians, which meant Great Island in their language."[18]

Meginness, in the same account, also reiterates that "Shawana Ben, chief of the remnant of the Shawanese, was, in 1768, also living at the Great Island, as he replied to a letter informing him of the murder of a number of his relatives on Middle Creek. The letter is very peculiar, and may be seen in Vol. IX., p. 480, *Colonial Records*.[19]

It seems apparent that Shawana Ben may have just been a corruption of the name Shawnee Ben, since he was a Shawnee chief. Whether or not his name was the name that Shoemaker chose to use on his monument for "Shawana" the supposed "Last Indian girl in the West Branch Valley" will always be a matter of speculation. It is suggestive, however, since no other historical references I've consulted make any reference to a last Indian girl of the West Branch Valley or to any Indian girl of that name.

An historical distortion like this is also something Shoemaker was prone to do when making up his own history of Pennsylvania. Tradition remains silent upon the matter, but if an Indian maiden is indeed buried here, her rest is undoubtedly a peaceful and pleasant one. The murmur of Nichols Run nearby offers soothing comfort night and day, as does the perfume

---

18. John F. Meginness, "History of the Great Island and William Dunn," *The Historical Journal, Volume II, Number 1*, 1894, 7.
19. Ibid.

Artist's rendition of Princess Shawana of Nichols Run and chief Wiidaagh of Antes Creek, Lycoming County. The two never met in real life. Photo courtesy of Jersey Shore Historical Society - artist's name not known.

of the surrounding forest. Heavily scented with pines and hemlocks after heavy rains, and with honeysuckle and spice bushes in the springtime, it is enough to quiet the spirits of any troubled soul.

Some Further Notes on Shawana's Grave:

a. In his *Otzinachson*, Meginness also mentions many other Indian burial places in the West Branch Valley (see pages 82-85), including Clinton Harbor, Reed's Hill, Lock Haven, Monsey Town Flats, Sterling Run, and others; but no mention of a grave along Nichol's Run.

b. There is one other Indian burial site that not only escaped the attention of historians but also of Henry Shoemaker. The names of the Indian chief and his Indian maiden that are said to be buried on the mountain above Picture Rocks have not come down to us, but their memory is preserved in the folktales of the area. Their resting place was also once marked by a brass plaque nailed to a tree growing over their graves.

Someone has stolen it in years past, but local tradition still preserves their memory (See chapter #8 titled "Picture Rocks," in the author's *Pennsylvania Mountain Landmarks Volume 1* for the interesting story about this forgotten place). In my humble opinion, this fact adds some credence to the idea that there may be some truth to the idea that there was once an Indian maiden buried at the Shawana gravesite.

c. The only Nichols name of any significance to this inquiry I could find was a mention of a Thomas Nichols, who was one of the first settlers in Porter Township of Lycoming County in the late eighteenth century, the same township where Jersey Shore and Nichols Run are found today. He is also listed as a County Commissioner of that county in 1812. Although many Pennsylvania placenames are based on the names of the person who first settled there, I could find no indications that this was the case for Nichols Run, which drains into Pine Creek at Jersey Shore. This fact, on the other hand, makes it interesting to note that Thomas Nichols is buried at Pine Creek Cemetery in Jersey Shore.[20]

7. John Goodaway's Sycamore: Sitting just off Linglestown Road in Dauphin County is a remarkable natural landmark. Said to be one of the largest trees in the state, the giant Sycamore attracts many local and out-of-state sightseers every year. What those visitors may not realize, however, is that this ancient survivor also serves as a memorial to a local Indian who is buried in a nearby grave site. But first, more about the tree.

It is thought to be at least 400 hundred years old and has been designated a "Champion Tree" by the Pennsylvania Forestry Association. Its dimensions, according to their Pennsylvania Champion Tree Program: height of 111 feet, circumference twenty-five and a half feet (diameter of eight feet), and a crown spread of 137 feet. Not many trees can claim dimensions of this magnitude, but in addition to its size (at one time claimed to be the fourth largest in the state), it is also noted for its unusual name.[21]

Its title was given to it by locals, probably after they buried John Goodaway in the shadows of its leafy branches. That they gave him last rites, a decent burial, and preserved his memory by bestowing his name upon the tree that overlooks his gravesite is a testament to the respect that they must

---

20. John F. Meginness, *History of Lycoming County*, Pennsylvania, 258.
21. https://www.pabigtrees.com/tree-listings/TR20101011185950933

Old photo of the John Goodaway Sycamore when it stood in an empty field and before nature began to reclaim the land around it. (Photo by Nevin W. Moyer, courtesy of Bill Minsker and the Lower Paxton Township Historical Commission)

have had for the man. History records that he was the last of the friendly Indians who lived in Central Pennsylvania and was the last of his race.[22]

Not much more is known about him, since neither his name nor his history is recorded in any local histories or in any well-known historical references on Pennsylvania's Native Americans. Even Nevin W. Moyer, the prolific and highly respected Dauphin County historian, never wrote anything about John Goodaway other than referencing the man's burial site.[23]

It is easy to speculate, however, that as the last of his tribe, Goodaway's loneliness had to be unbearable at times, and his grief must have been just as overwhelming when he remembered how the final peaceful remnants of his tribe had been cruelly and indiscriminately murdered (men, women, and children alike). Those homicidal killings occurred during two bloody raids at Conestoga Indian Town and subsequently at the Lancaster County Jail in Lancaster County on December 14 and December 27, 1763.

---

22. https://www.atlasobscura.com/places/john-goodway-sycamore-tree. Also described in a newspaper article titled "Biggest Tree in Pennsylvania Discovered on John Early Farm," *The Bourbon News*, Paris, Kentucky, December 3, 1920. See also https://www.abc27.com/digital-originals/the-awe-inspiring-goodaway-sycamore-we-have-a-very-large-tree-in-the-back/

23. William Minsker, nephew of Nevin W. Moyer, email dated January 2, 2025.

Photo of the John Goodaway Sycamore as it looks today. (Taken by the author in June of 2025)

The perpetrators were the infamous Paxtang Rangers, also known as the Paxton Boys, from Dauphin County. For years they had been the victims of many bloody raids on their homesteads by Indian war parties since the onset of the French and Indian War in 1757 and in subsequent years. Suspecting the innocent Conestogas as being complicit in the raids, the rangers vowed revenge and their subsequent actions remain a black mark on the otherwise honest and sturdy pioneers of Dauphin County, and a sad chapter in the many heroic deeds of the local rangers known as the Paxton Boys.[24] See the chapter titled "God's Warriors" in the author's *Pennsylvania Fireside Tales volumes 4* and *8* for photos and details about this shameful event.

HISTORICAL CONTRADICTION:

According to one source, John Goodaway may not have been the last of his tribe after all. Apparently, there was at one time "a tradition in Brecknock Township, Lancaster County, that one of the Conestoga Indians who had

---

24. Paul A. W. Wallace, *Indians in Pennsylvania*, 152–53; Jack Brubaker, *Massacre of the Conestogas: On the Trail of the Paxton Boys in Lancaster County*, American Heritage Magazine, November 26, 2010; Helen Hunt Jackson, "Massacres of Indians by whites—The Conestoga Massacre," *A Century of Dishonor, Chapter IX*, 298–324.

Closeup of the large trunk of the John Goodaway Sycamore, with my white baseball cap laid at its base for perspective. (Taken by the author in June of 2025)

escaped both massacres was secretly given protection for the rest of his life on a farm near Alleghenyville."[25]

The account, (which appears in the Pennsylvania Archives, 2nd Series II, p 739) explains that "It is known for certain that two elderly Indians from Conestoga survived, having been living as servants on the farm of Christian Hershey in Warwick Township of Lancaster County at the time of the massacre. A few months later they were given a safe conduct, dated August 17, 1764."[26]

The safe conduct document they carried explained that the bearers, "Michael and Mary, his wife, were friendly Indians of the Delaware tribe, who formerly resided with other Indians in the Conestoga Manor, and that they had for the past fifteen months or more, been living with Christian Hershey at his plantation in Warwick Township, Lancaster County. All persons were called upon to treat them with civility and to afford them all necessary assistance."[27]

---

25. Ibid.
26. Ibid.
27. Ibid.

Where John Goodaway's grave might be. Supposedly about ten feet or more north of the tree, but now densely overgrown with cone flowers and other weeds which are entangled with fallen tree branches and twigs.

NOTES:
Despite extensive historical research, I could not find any mention of John Goodaway in any historical records of Dauphin County. That includes Sipe's *Indian Chiefs*, Montgomery's *Frontier Forts*, Kelker's *History of Dauphin County*, and Egle's *Notes & Queries—Chiefly Relating to the History of Dauphin County*. If it wasn't for the oral history of the area that has been handed down through the ages, John Goodaway would be a forgotten man, lost in the mists that sometimes dance over his gravesite under that great sycamore tree along Linglestown Road.

John Goodaway's gravesite is located about 400 yards east of Fort Gilchrist, one of the last surviving frontier refuges in the state (see Chapter 7, "Survivors of Pennsylvania's Frontier Days"). It seems like an ironic twist of fate that the last Native American in the area, who was so peaceful and was so friendly to his white neighbors, is buried near a place that was built to protect the valley's early settlers from Indian attacks.

BIBLIOGRAPHY

Baer, Christopher T., *A General Chronology of the Pennsylvania Railroad Company Predecessors and Successors and its Historical Context*, Pennsylvania Railroad Historical and Technical Society, Columbus, Ohio, October 2015.
Beers, J. H., *Historical and Biographical Annals of Columbia and Montour Counties, Pennsylvania*, J. H. Beers and Company, Chicago, 1915.
Beck, Doctor William F., *History of The Beck Family and Their Descendants Everywhere Including Bucks, Graziers, Nearfhoofs and Kriders, the Pioneer Settlers of Warriors Mark Valley, 1768 to 1940*. The Commercial Printing Company, Altoona, PA, July 1942.
Brubaker, John H., *Massacre of the Conestogas: on the Trail of the Paxton Boys in Lancaster County*, History Press, Charleston, South Carolina, 2010.
Day, Sherman, *Historical Collections of the State of Pennsylvania*, Ira J. Friedman, Port Washington, NY, 1843.
Doddridge, Joseph, *Notes on the Settlement and Indian Wars of the Western Parts of Virginia and Pennsylvania*, Ritenour and Lindsey, Pittsburgh, 1912.
Donehoo, Doctor George P., *Indian Villages and Place Names in Pennsylvania*, Gateway Press, Baltimore, 1977.
Egle, William H., *Notes and Queries—Chiefly Relating to the History of Dauphin County, Pennsylvania*, Telegraph Press, Harrisburg, Pennsylvania, 1881–1883.
Ellis, Franklin, and Austin N. Hungerford, editors, *History of that Part of the Susquehanna and Juniata Valleys Embraced in the Counties of Mifflin, Juniata, Perry, Union and Snyder, in the Commonwealth of Pennsylvania*, Everts, Peck and Richards, Philadelphia, 1886.
Espenshade, A. Howry, *Pennsylvania Place Names*, The Evangelical Press, Harrisburg, Pennsylvania, 1925.
Fisher, Forest K., *It Happened in Mifflin County, Book 2*, Mifflin County Historical Society, Lewistown, Pennsylvania, 2005.
Futhey, J. Smith and Cope, Gilbert, *History of Chester County Pennsylvania*, Louis H. Everts, Philadelphia, 1881.
Grumet, Robert S., *Northeastern Indian Lives, 1632-1816*, University of Massachusetts Press, Amherst, MA, 1996.

Heckewelder, Reverend John, *History, Manner, and Customs of the Indian Nations*, Lippincott's Press, Philadelphia, 1876.

Heckewelder, Reverend John and Peter S. Du Ponceau, *Names Which the Lenni Lenape or Delaware Indians, etc.*, Transactions of the American Philosophical Society, Volume 4, article 11, American Philosophical Society, 1799.

Hunter, William A., *Forts on the Pennsylvania Frontier 1753–1758*, Pennsylvania Historical and Museum Commission, Harrisburg, Pennsylvania, 1960.

Hodge, Frederick Webb, *Handbook of American Indians North of Mexico*, The Smithsonian Institution, Bureau of American Ethnology Handbook of American Indians, Washington, 1912.

Ignoffo, Mary Jo, *Captive of the Labyrinth: Sarah L. Winchester, Heiress of the Rifle Fortune*, University of Missouri Press, Columbia, Missouri, 2010.

Imhof, John D., Elk County—A Journey Through Time, Volume One, Baumgratz Publishing, St. Marys, Pennsylvania, 2019.

Ingram, John H., *The Haunted Homes and Family Traditions of Great Britain*, Reeves and Turner Company, London, 1905.

Irving, Washington, *The Life of George Washington*, John Murray, London, 1856.

Jackson, Helen Hunt, *A Century of Dishonor*, Harper and Brothers, New York, 1885.

Jones, Richard, Haunted Britain and Ireland, New Holland Publishers, London, 2003.

Jones, Uriah J., *History of the Early Settlement of the Juniata Valley*, Telegraph Press, Harrisburg, 1889.

Karns, C. W., *Historical Sketches of Morrison's Cove*, Mirror Press, Altoona, Pennsylvania, 1933.

Kelker, Luther R., *History of Dauphin County, Pennsylvania*, Lewis Publishing Company, New York, 1907.

Linn, John Blair, *History of Centre and Clinton Counties, Pennsylvania*, Louis H. Everts Company, Philadelphia, 1883.

Loudon, Archibald, *A Selection of Some of the Most Interesting Narratives of Outrages Committed by the Indians in their wars with the White People*, A. Loudon Press, Carlisle, PA, 1808.

Meginness, John F., *Otzinachson, A History of the West Branch Valley*, Gazette and Bulletin Printing House, Williamsport, Pennsylvania, 1889.

———, *History of the Great Island and William Dunn, Its Owner, and Founder of Dunnstown*, Gazette and Bulletin Printing House, Williamsport, Pennsylvania, 1894.

Meginness, John F., *History of Lycoming County Pennsylvania*, Brown, Runk and Company Publishers, Chicago, 1892.

Merrell, James H., Into the American Woods, Negotiators on the American Frontier, Norton and Company, New York, 1999.

Meyers, Albert, *Narratives of Early Pennsylvania, West New Jersey, and Delaware 1630-1007*, Charles Scribner's Sons, New York, 1912.

MacReynolds, George, *Place Names in Bucks County, Pennsylvania*, Bucks County Historical Society, Doylestown, Pennsylvania, 1942.

Montgomery, Thomas L., editor, *Frontier Forts of Pennsylvania*, Pennsylvania Historical Commission, Harrisburg, PA, 1916.

Pollard, Albert F., contributor, "West, Thomas (1577–1618)," *Dictionary of National Biography*, Smith, Elder, and Company, London, 1900.

Pritts, Joseph, *Mirror of Olden Time Border Life*, S. S. Miles, Abingdon, Virginia, 1849.

Rosenberger, Homer Tope, *Mountain Folks*, Annie H. Ross Library, Lock Haven, Pennsylvania, 1974.

Schell, Hon. W. P., *Annals of Bedford County*, Self-published booklet "For Old Home Week," Bedford, Pennsylvania, August 4, 1907.

Shoemaker, Henry W., *Eldorado Found*, Altoona Tribune Publishing Co., Altoona, Pennsylvania, 1917.

Sipe, C. Hale, *The Indian Chiefs of Pennsylvania*, Ziegler Printing Company, Butler, PA, 1927.

———, *The Indian Wars of Pennsylvania*, The Telegraph Press, Harrisburg, PA, 1931.

Smith, James, *An Account of the Remarkable Occurrences in the Life and Travels of Col. James Smith*, John Bradford, Lexington KY, 1799.

Stewart, J. T., *History of Indiana County Pennsylvania, Volume 1*, J. H. Beers and Company, Chicago, 1913.

Taber, Thomas T. III, *Railroads of Pennsylvania Encyclopedia and Atlas*, Self-published, Muncy, Pennsylvania, 1987.

Wallace, Paul A. W., *Indians in Pennsylvania*, Pennsylvania Historical and Museum Commission, Harrisburg, Pennsylvania, 1961.

———, *Indians Paths of Pennsylvania*, Pennsylvania Historical and Museum Commission, Harrisburg, PA, 1965.

Waterman and Watkins, *History of Bedford, Somerset, and Fulton Counties, Pennsylvania*, Waterman and Watkins, Chicago, 1884.

Weslager, Clinton A., *The Delaware Indians: A History*, Rutgers University Press, New Brunswick, NJ, 1972.

Withers, Alexander Scott, *Chronicles of Border Warfare*, 2010 reprint by Leonaur Publishing Company, Edinburgh, Scotland, of the first edition published by Joseph Israel Publishing, Clarksburg, VA, 1831.

Williams, Michael, *Deforesting the Earth*, University of Chicago Press, Chicago, 2002.

ABOUT THE AUTHOR

JEFFREY R. FRAZIER was born and raised in Centre Hall, Centre County, where he says he grew up in a "Tom Sawyer sort of way", later graduating with a BS from Penn State in 1967, and then with an MBA from Rider University in New Jersey in 1978. Some of the fondest memories of his boyhood include explorations of out-of-the-way spots in the mountains and accounts of the legends that seem to cling to them, and beginning in 1970 he began collecting those same kind of anecdotes from all over the state; ranging from the Blue Mountains of Berks and Lehigh Counties, the South Mountains of Adams County, the "Black Forest" area of Potter and Tioga Counties, the Alleghenies of Clearfield and Blair Counties, and the other counties in the middle. He has compiled his vast collection of tales into a series titled *Pennsylvania Fireside Tales*. The *Pennsylvania Mountain Landmarks* series is a continuation of his work, written in a format that the average reader can enjoy, especially those who love the green valleys and cloud-covered mountain peaks of Pennsylvania as much as he does.

www.ingramcontent.com/pod-product-compliance
Lightning Source LLC
Chambersburg PA
CBHW010855090426
42737CB00019B/3380